ACCOLADE

Every relationship has pivot points where a difficult conversation is inevitable—including our relationship with God. But how can we have a DTR (Define the Relationship) with the Divine? Sarah tackles this topic with her typical wit and grace. *Hey God, Can We Talk?* is a template for honesty with God when it matters most.

Mark E. Moore, PhD
Author, *Core 52*
Teaching Pastor, Christ's Church of the Valley

My friend Sarah Bowling has written a book that will bring you into a closer relationship with God than you have ever known. Here is a no-nonsense book that is designed to honor God—both the Word and Spirit—and will bring you joy. If it is intimacy with the Spirit you want, this is your book.

R. T. Kendall
Author, *Total Forgiveness*

Jesus is the Vine and we are the branches. All fruitfulness flows from intimacy with Him. To grow in intimacy and bear fruit, we need to hear God's voice and follow His ways. Sarah Bowling is a faithful friend of Jesus with a huge heart for the Body of Christ. Her book *Hey God, Can We Talk?* provides step-by-step methods to hear His voice. Sarah delves deeply into the lives of biblical heroes, vulnerably shares her story, and interviews friends to present many ways of building relationship with God. I am grateful for Sarah's life and for her passion to help everyone hear God's voice. Read this book, find yourself in the story, and experiment with the Conversation Starters. I pray God will speak to you clearly as you find the model that is right for you. You are created for intimacy and fruitfulness!

Heidi G. Baker, PhD
Iris Global Cofounder and Executive Chairman of the Board

How do I talk with God? As a pastor for more than forty years, I can affirm that this is one of the most frequently asked questions from those who want to have a deeper relationship with God. This book not only provides the practical how-to help for conversing with God, but is also firmly rooted in the stories of Scripture. Sarah's enthusiasm and life experience make for a compelling and life-changing read. Start talking with God today.

Dianne Leman
Founding Pastor, The Vineyard Church of Central Illinois

Sarah is a deep well, and her love for people can be felt in the pages of her book, *Hey God, Can We Talk?* Talking to God can leave us with a sense of overwhelm, underwhelm, or even loneliness; and while Sarah acknowledges the challenges we face in learning to engage with God, she encourages us to grow in our dialogue with ourselves, God, and others. Rather than commands, monologues, or one-sided relationships, we can learn from Scripture and our personal experience how to lean into reciprocal, honest, and fulfilling relationships. Whatever your faith tradition, this book will help you on your journey, and is a great gift for friends.

Ashley Abercrombie
Author, *Rise of the Truth Teller*
Cohost, Why Tho Podcast

Sarah writes from the deepest places of the heart and soul. If you struggle to know how to talk to God when life makes no sense, here is a powerful conversation starter.

Sheila Walsh
Author, TV Host, Bible Teacher

HEY GOD,
CAN WE TALK?

DESTINY IMAGE BOOKS BY SARAH BOWLING

How to Keep Your Faith in an Upside Down World

HEY GOD, CAN WE TALK?

REAL-LIFE GOD ENCOUNTERS FOR REAL-LIFE CIRCUMSTANCES

SARAH BOWLING

DESTINY IMAGE® PUBLISHERS, INC.
P.O. Box 310, Shippensburg, PA 17257-0310
"Promoting Inspired Lives."

This book and all other Destiny Image and Destiny Image Fiction books are available at Christian bookstores and distributors worldwide.

Cover design by Eileen Rockwell.

For more information on foreign distributors, call 717-532-3040.

Reach us on the Internet: www.destinyimage.com.

ISBN 13 TP: 978-0-7684-5573-1

ISBN 13 eBook: 978-0-7684-5574-8

ISBN 13 HC: 978-0-7684-5576-2

ISBN 13 LP: 978-0-7684-5575-5

For Worldwide Distribution, Printed in the U.S.A.

1 2 3 4 5 6 7 8 / 25 24 23 22 21

I dedicate this book to Encounter Church in Denver. I deeply treasure and appreciate my church family—their grace, generosity, encouragement, and affording me the opportunity to explore these conversations with you on Wednesday nights!

ACKNOWLEDGMENTS

There are heaps and heaps of folks who deserve recognition for this project—for their support, encouragement, investment, patience, basement for writing, listening ears, and gracious wisdom. Thank you so very much for your wonderful teamwork: Mrs. Giovanetti, Encounter Church, Nathan Foster, Tyler Duffus, Dustin Groeneman, Dave Reiter, Lori Janke, Shaun Tabatt, Brian Welch, Richard Foster, and my enduring family. Thank you so very much!

CONTENTS

FOREWORD

God made us for connection and communication. We are wired for it, and our life of spending time reading the Bible helps us to access our spiritual journey of talking to God. This book is going to help redefine your times of prayer and connection with God. It will help to set your expectation for a new normal. It will also bring you into some honest self-awareness about your own heart and how to present it to God in a way that is authentic as well.

Hearing from God has sometimes been looked at as an art or talent—only certain people are gifted enough for it unless it's an emergency. God is helping us to grasp what He wanted all along—connection and communication. He created us to know His perceptions and thoughts about our world. I love what Paul says in First Corinthians 2 where

Paul is basically giving us the keys to communication with God. He shares in verse 9 about how the Holy Spirit shows us what no man would normally see. On top of this, the Spirit looks into the deepest parts of God's perspective and shares it with us. He finishes it with a profound thought:

> *For who has ever intimately known the mind of the Lord Yahweh well enough to become his counselor? Christ has, and we possess Christ's perceptions* (1 Corinthians 2:16 The Passion Translation).

Isn't that an amazing thought? We, as children of God filled with His Spirit, have the perceptions of Christ. As we learn how to converse with Him through His Spirit about the hardest and most beautiful parts of life, we will know Him in a way that changes our very real day-to-day existence. I am not just convinced of this; I have lived it, and His deep talks with me have changed my own life's outcome. I am not a self-made man limited to my skills, talents, and intelligence alone, but I have had an outcome based on walking out a very personal relationship with the Spirit of God. I could not have gotten the satisfaction out of my marriage, family, career, and ministry without being shaped by very real conversations with God. It was a two-way street, as love should be. We all go through periods of feeling its one-sided, or we want to hear God more than He wants to speak, but it couldn't be further from the truth. As you learn to honestly talk with God, you will come to realize over and over that He really did initiate the hunger and desire inside of you and He has been pursuing you far deeper than you have pursued Him.

The encouraging thing is we are never too young or old to start walking this out. One of the first real conversations I remember having with God was when I was 13 years old (yes, I was young). I had been raised by Christian parents and I had borrowed their faith and believed it, but I was really ready for my own connection to God to define what my real faith journey was. I was on a soccer field at practice and there was a new kid everyone didn't like because he was so socially awkward. I remember hearing right past my own thoughts, internally: "Go talk to him; he is not who you think he is. He is just really broken and afraid."

I remember saying, "But if I go talk to him everyone will make fun of me; he is so awkward!" and I didn't go that day. I felt really guilty about it over the weekend and didn't know how to talk to God after the first real thing I felt He was asking I wouldn't do, so finally I said, "What do I *not* see that you want to show me?"

It was a simple question, but it's like I borrowed a glimpse of God's love for this kid in my mind's eye, and I couldn't see the pain and rejection, the awkward behavior, the social issues. I was instead seeing a fighter, a leader, an athlete, and a friend. The next week when practice came, I befriended him, and yes, I was made fun of, but now my reputation didn't matter because I had talked to God about this kid and he wasn't who people thought he was. He ended up being my best friend for years. He was an amazing athlete, a great comedian, and really fun to have adventures with. It ruined me for having real conversations with God. I wanted to know more of what He thought that I wasn't in touch with.

I love the author of this book, Sarah, and her authenticity. She has provided an incredible series of conversation starters through this book. I have needed tools all through my own spiritual growth journey, but I wish this one was here sooner! I have, though, grabbed tools throughout the years to add to my own conversation with God, and they have accelerated so much for me and have helped me avoid the frustration that so many talk about in their personal prayer pursuit of God. This book is so valuable, and I think of my own need, like sometimes out of deep pain or betrayal I needed someone else to help take the lead through their devotional, book, therapy or expression. Other times, when I was learning to really connect to something about God that I was uncomfortable with (like sharing my faith), I needed other written and media tools to help form my own language between the Spirit and my heart.

Ultimately, many Christians will not have the deep or hard conversations with God unless they are in shutdown mode or need breakthrough because they just lack faith that He is that personal and practical, but He is. And there is this book to help you grow into a place of fulfillment in this relationship with God that He has wired you for. Sarah has made it attainable for you, so grab hold of your seat belt—your life is about to change drastically!

Read this book and dive deep into God's mind, heart, and perceptions that you get to share through our Christian heritage.

Shawn Bolz

1

WHAT'S A CONVERSATION WITH GOD?

"Stop taking your anger out on me! I'm not the one you're mad at. It's the other pothead snowboarders who are the reckless and dangerous jerks on the slopes!" This was my retort to a really angry dad who was giving me an earful after his 5'8" son, who was learning to ski, collided with me as I was snowboarding down a mountain.

This dad was cussing up a storm in front of his son and two of my kids. I made an impulsive decision to stand up for myself because I hadn't done anything wrong. I also could tell that this dad thought that I was the typical, irresponsible snowboarder who had been flying recklessly down the mountain, who was possibly high on weed, who had been oblivious to anyone else on the slope, and who was possibly mowing down newbies for sport.

"I'm a forty-four-year-old mom who has three kids in elementary school and two of them are just behind you! I appreciate that you're protective of your son, but he turned suddenly into me as I was snowboarding past him. This was an accidental collision." I could tell that my words had struck a chord in his thoughts.

He replied to me, "You're right. I'm mad at the other reckless snowboarders on the mountain and I took my anger out on you. Please forgive me."

"Of course! I'm mad at them too, and I understand why you're ticked off! It's no problem. I'm glad your son isn't hurt. Have a really enjoyable and safe day of skiing and enjoying some family time."

This conversation with a total stranger turned out pretty well, even though it started off highly volatile. Why do we have conversations? What are some possible purposes for talking with someone? Before we identify some purposes and goals for conversations, it would be helpful to define what a conversation is as well as what a conversation is not.

MONOLOGUE, COMMAND, OR INFORMATION DOWNLOAD

For starters, a conversation is not a command. If I tell one of my kids, "Please switch the laundry from the washer to the dryer," or, "Please do your homework," I am commanding or requiring these actions from my kids. This is one form of communication, and there is not much room for push-back or discussion.

In the Bible, there are lots of times when God commands someone to do or not do something. For example, Genesis 2:16-17 says, *"The Lord God commanded the man saying, 'From any tree of the garden you may eat freely; but from the tree of knowledge of good and evil you shall not eat, for in the day that you eat from it you will surely die.'"* There is no input or feedback from Adam in the subsequent verses, and none is requested. More examples of the command form of communication can be seen in what God says to Noah in Genesis 7–8 and as the Ten Commandments are given (see Exodus 20).

Another example of what a conversation is not is the monologue form of communication. "Monologue" is a Greek compound word comprised of the words *mono* and *logue*. In the Greek, *mono* is the word for alone or single, and *logue* is the word for speak, speech or word.[1] A monologue is when someone speaks to you and there is no space for your input or feedback. This can be a transfer of information, like when a teacher gives a lecture, when you hear a sermon, or when the flight attendant tells you about the location of the emergency exits on your aircraft during the safety orientation. If we are not careful, we can get into the bad habit of using a monologue as our primary communication form with our kids, spouse, coworkers, friends, etc. While a monologue can be helpful to transfer information, it is not very relational or conversational, nor is it an effective method for cultivating connection or a close relationship.

For example, I had a relationship with a person who was well-versed in a particular subject, and this person was keen to tell me all about the vast array of personal experience and education on that subject. Because I can be a good listener, the relationship seemed to be semi-close. But after some time, it became clear to me that my role in the relationship as a listener only facilitated the other person's role as an expert. Our "conversations" didn't have a give-and-take rhythm or flow. Instead, all of the talking was more like a monologue. As I reflect on this relationship, I am saddened because it lasted for a season, but didn't facilitate a close connection beyond the transfer of information.

What is a conversation? The word "conversation" comes from the Latin root words *con* and *versare*. *Con* is the Latin prefix that means "with or together" and *versare* means "to turn."[2] The idea of conversation is to turn together. Some synonyms for conversation include dialogue, converse, exchange, or discuss. In a conversation, communication goes back and forth with participants turning together for talking, listening, mutual participation, interaction, and dialogue.

To this end, there can be lots of purposes for conversations. These include debate, witty banter, facilitating an accomplishment or project, clearing up miscommunication, staying current with or deepening a relationship, and discussing a topic of mutual interest. The process of considering the various purposes for conversations can help us align our expectations of what we can expect to either bring or receive from a conversation.

I recently had an interesting conversation with a long-time college friend. I learned that she had been diagnosed with cancer, and her struggle to overcome this terrible disease wasn't going well. I happened to be visiting her city and wanted to spend some time with her. When I learned that she was in the hospital, I texted to see if she would be up for a visit. She eagerly replied, "YES!" I was super happy to get to see her and to catch up with some wonderful one-on-one time. In fact, during my stay in her city, I was able to visit her several times.

On one of my visits, she explained that the doctors had just told her that they had run out of options for treating the cancer. They were losing this battle. I could already see by her condition, the medical equipment, and the attention that she was receiving that her health was truly declining.

Upon telling me this information, she asked, "Sarah, what do you think about what the doctors are telling me?" Even as I write this today, I'm still unraveled by this question. When she asked me this, I paused for quite some time. My eyes welled with tears, the pit in my stomach grew, and I fondly remembered our fun, deep, witty, compassionate, and vulnerable conversations back in our college days. I thought about her kids, siblings, parents, and the people in her life for whom this devastating news would have an effect.

"Well my friend," I replied through my tears as I held her hand, "that doesn't sound like very good information. How do you feel about what they're saying?"

She replied, "Of course I don't like what they're saying, and I've fought this battle for several years now." She continued

23

to talk about various possibilities, her kids, familial relationships, and what this information could mean for the next part of her life. In our conversation, she was honest with me, and I was present with her. As we shared our feelings, the pain of the doctors' news was processed through the deep connection that we had.

I share this story because it expresses some possibilities for what conversations can facilitate. If our earthly conversations can facilitate such deep connections and exchanges between humans, how much more can our conversations with God serve to deepen our relationship with our Creator?

The purpose of this book is to help guide you in your conversations with God, to show you how to have a deeper and more intimate connection with Him, and to assist you in knowing Him better through various kinds of conversations. To accomplish this, I have selected a few Bible characters who had conversations with God at important milestones in their lives. I have selected conversations that include elements of communication that are virtually universal to our human existence. These conversations include a wide array of experiences that include making major life decisions, going through a total life meltdown, envisioning a hopeless future, failing God, and more.

How do you talk with God about difficult life issues? How does God talk and dialogue with you in these experiences? This book helps you face difficult conversations with God, with the ultimate goal that you grow closer and more intimate with Him.

The Bible characters I have chosen are imperfect and relatable, because I appreciate that you and I are flawed and frail humans. We are all leading lives that include mistakes, unexpected events, interactions with other flawed people, and our own misguided perceptions. Their relatability will help us as we explore the various conversations that we can have with God.

CONVERSATION STARTERS

In addition to the biblical examples of these conversations, each chapter contains a section called Conversation Starters. These sections are designed to give you tools for having deep, meaningful, and connecting conversations with God. For many reasons, I believe that these sections are extremely important. Sometimes we can be so overwhelmed in a season or experience that we can't find appropriate words for communicating or conversing. The Conversation Starters that I suggest can be very helpful in terms of giving a starting point, some practical direction, and sometimes a map— or at least some mile markers for conversations.

Additionally, we can sometimes get in ruts regarding how we communicate with God. A conversation rut can be when we get stuck in the request mode and forget about the dialogue nature of a conversation. It can look like praying the Lord's Prayer but neglecting to be present. For some people, having a conversation with God feels as foreign as attempting to talk with an alien. For all these reasons, I am including some helpful ways to both start a conversation with God and to facilitate an ongoing dialogue with Him.

I feel that these sections are essential to cultivating growth in your walk with God. Because of the nature of these Conversation Starters, I strongly encourage you to try them one at a time over the course of several weeks or months. These exercises can sometimes take a little practice before you are comfortable with a new way of conversing. Additionally, I have found that each of these Conversation Starters accentuates a unique experience that creates depth with God. Some are more comfortable and natural for me, while others take more discipline and work. But I can say with full confidence that each of these Conversation Starters has been a vital part of my ever-deepening walk with God.

Several years ago, I heard a sermon in church that taught about praying along with the Lord's Prayer. The sermon was very inspiring, and it challenged me to pray the Lord's Prayer for one hour based on Jesus' question to His disciples in Gethsemane, *"Could you not tarry one hour?"* (see Matthew 26:40). I was very motivated to implement this prayer pattern into my daily routine. The next day, I set aside one hour and attempted to pray the Lord's Prayer.

It was awful. After three minutes I checked my watch, entirely convinced that I had already clocked off twelve minutes on my way to sixty minutes. Needless to say, I was very discouraged, and I quickly concluded that I was unable to tarry with Jesus for one hour, just like His disciples had failed back in Gethsemane. I completely gave up trying. A couple of decades later, I was motivated again to use the Lord's

Prayer as a Conversation Starter. This time, though, I did it in more of a conversational manner. I realized quickly how much life and vibrancy was available for me in this conversation with God.

I have had many conversations with God over the years. These started when I was very young. I grew up a pastor's kid, so church was my second home. I remember wandering the halls of our church when I was four or five years old talking with God and experiencing God talking with me. It felt very normal and natural to me. We talked when I would meander into the quiet and empty sanctuary and pause to soak in the warmth and peaceful stillness of that room. As an adult looking back, I recognize that these conversations and experiences with God helped to shape my awareness of talking and listening to Him.

As I got older, I had conversations with God on long walks or on bicycle rides on nearby nature trails. God and I would talk together as I walked in the creek behind my house. We would work through friendship struggles, talk about my desire to fit in with my peers at school, etc., all as I reflected on His handiwork that I experienced in the nature that surrounded us. When I think back, I am very grateful that my childhood was directed and influenced by these conversations.

Jesus tells us that we must come to God as children—simple, honest, vulnerable, active, and enthusiastic! So, let's begin this wonderful adventure and see what conversations we can explore and enjoy with God as we become transformed through the dialogue.

ENDNOTES

1. Douglas Harper, "Monologue," Online Etymology Dictionary, https:etymonline.com/search?q=monologue; accessed May 11, 2020.

2. Douglas Harper, "Converse," Online Etymology Dictionary, https://www.etymonline.com/search?q=converse; accessed May 11, 2020.

2

CAN WE TALK—
I ROYALLY SCREWED UP

"I don't believe that Jesus is the Son of God." Since I grew up as a pastor's kid, I had a massively hard time sharing this statement with my folks. It was even more challenging because when I shared this with them, I was about to finish my senior year in college, and I feared that my parents might cut off their financial support for my schooling.

Furthermore, I feared that my words would be hurtful and cut deeply into my mom's sense of propriety. I was nervous about how she might react when I unzipped my heart and was completely honest. I scheduled this difficult conversation with my parents in a public restaurant hoping that the neutral location would soften the blow. I was greatly relieved when they responded very well to my difficult news.

"Sarah, we loved you when you were a baby and you didn't believe anything. This love hasn't changed, and we continue to love you regardless of what you believe." My mom went on to say that she knew I was on a faith journey, and she was confident that God would help me find Jesus again. Needless to say, I was abundantly relieved by her response, and I entered my senior year of college continuing to explore various religious traditions and faiths.

This exploration led me to consider Islam, Hinduism, Buddhism, and Christianity. To make a long story short, I read *Mere Christianity* by C. S. Lewis and was very attracted to a faith that was grounded in a loving God. After several months of exploring and wrestling with various spiritual questions, I decided to put my faith in Jesus.

One evening shortly after this journey, I had an intimate encounter with God where I felt His love in a really powerful and tangible way. Feeling God's love in that moment was like wave after wave of warmth, tenderness, gentleness, and compassion washing over me, accepting and soothing my orphan soul. What made this even more special was that I recognized that God's love for me had not changed, even when I had walked away from Him to explore other faith traditions. I melted into a puddle of tears, snuggled under my blanket, and fell asleep with the overwhelming assurance that, even though I had walked away from Him, He still loved me.

I share this experience with you as a starting point to talk about the conversations we can have with God when we mess up, walk away from Him, question our faith, struggle with personal issues, and lots more. This is important because all of us screw up in a wide variety of ways, and no one is exempt from being human or flawed, or from struggling with weaknesses, questions, mistakes, and fail-ures. And when we royally screw up with God, it can be really difficult to navigate some of the potholes and landmines in our faith journey, let alone have any kind of constructive con-versation with Him. But there is lots of hope for us when we blow it with God based on the very first conversations in the Bible that happen between God and man.

If you think about it, Adam screwed up royally. God told him not to eat from the Tree of the Knowledge of Good and Evil, but he disobeyed. Prior to this decision, Adam and Eve had lived in paradise! There was abundant food, an ease of living, the absence of shame, a peaceful rhythm to life, and a constructive alignment with God. When Adam and Eve screwed up, everything began to unravel. So, what does a conversation with God look like when we royally screw up?

Let's appreciate that the very first documented conver-sation between God and man happened after Adam dis-obeyed God. God did talk with Adam before he messed up, but it was not conversational in the sense of dialogue between God and Adam. God had given Adam instructions about taking care of the Garden of Eden, and He gave him clear boundaries about eating from the Tree of the Knowl-edge of Good and Evil. The first time we see any dialogue or discussion between God and man is *after* Adam messed up.

I want to make this point clear to you, my dear reader, because we can often have the mindset that our conversa-tions with God are the deepest and most fruitful when we are walking in proper alignment and when our relationship with God is on the straight and narrow. But the conversation between God and Adam does not confirm that line of thinking.

Furthermore, how Adam behaved after he screwed up can also mirror some of our actions and mindsets when we mess up. Consider what Adam and Eve did in Genesis 3:7-8 immediately after they ate the forbidden fruit.

> *Then the eyes of both of them were opened, and they knew that they were naked; and they sewed fig leaves together and made themselves loin coverings. They heard the sound of the Lord God walking in the garden in the cool of the day, and the man and his wife hid themselves from the presence of the Lord God among the trees of the garden.*

In these verses, we read that Adam and Eve recognized that they were naked and felt ashamed, so they tried to cover themselves. When they heard God walking through the Garden, they hid because they were afraid of Him. It is noteworthy to think about Adam and Eve hiding from God, because we often behave the same way with God when we screw up. We can feel ashamed, unworthy, scared, uncomfortable, or inadequate, and we want to distance or hide ourselves from Him. We can stop attending a Bible study, conveniently forget to do a daily quiet time, immerse ourselves in the daily demands of a busy life, get slack on going to church, or any number of other behaviors that we might employ to create distance from God. These are some ways that we hide from God in our modern living.

Despite our efforts to create distance from God when we screw up, God seeks us out to converse with us for restoring connection and communication. God's behavior in the Garden of Eden toward Adam and Eve demonstrates this principle. *"Then the Lord God called to the man, and said to him, 'Where are you?'"* (Genesis 3:9). Let's take a few moments to consider both what God said and what He did not say in this verse.

God could have said some very truthful and even harsh things like, "I made this whole garden for you, Adam, and I gave you one small instruction that you didn't keep." And God could have asked lots of reasonable questions like:

- "How could you screw this up so massively?"
- "Why couldn't you follow My one instruction?"
- "What have you done?"
- "What's wrong with you?"
- "Who do you think you are, disobeying My one instruction?"

In God's question to Adam, *"Where are you?"* it looks as if God is endeavoring to find Adam even though God knows exactly where Adam is. Indeed, among all the choices of questions God could ask, He asks the most relational question possible. God already knows the answers to all these questions, and it was not God's intent to make Adam defensive, shamed, ostracized, berated, or belittled. The "where" question is neither condemning nor dismissive. The question that God asks Adam is meant to communicate to him that God is looking for him and wants him to stop hiding or pulling away from Him.

When we screw up with God, we should remember that God does not want us to hide from Him. Instead, He wants to be present with us and to talk about what happened. Even when we mess up, God wants to reconcile us to Himself. That is who God is—genuine love.

Maybe the best example I have seen of God's genuine love relates to a married couple I have known for decades. When I first got to know this couple, I had no idea that the husband was struggling with sexual addiction. I really enjoyed how practical this couple was, their humor, and their passion for God. Over the course of time, I learned about the husband's addiction, his struggles, and his journey out of this terrible captivity. In the husband's journey to freedom and the wife's process of healing her heart, they both experienced genuine love along each step of their recovery process, including the healing of wounds and identity restoration. Today when I talk with this couple, it is clear to me that they live in God's love. They are aware of their past and present struggles; but more importantly, they soak in God's love for them. God's love oozes out of them, full stop.

In addition to being able to see God's love redeem my friends, Adam's son, Cain, is another great example to study. Cain screwed up royally. It is possible that Cain's failure was even worse than Adam's, because in this instance, God intervened to try to stop Cain from messing up.

For a little backstory, Cain was a farmer. His brother, Abel, was a shepherd. Both brothers brought an offering to God that reflected their profession. Cain's offering was fruits and vegetables from his harvest. In contrast, Abel's offering was an animal from his flock. We read in Genesis 4:4-5 that God had regard for Abel's offering but was not impressed with what Cain had offered. This made Cain upset.

And this is where God steps into the struggle and tries to prevent Cain from doing something rash by attempting to start a potentially constructive conversation. God speaks to Cain and says,

> *Why are you angry? And why has your countenance fallen? If you do well, will not your countenance be lifted up? And if you do not do well, sin is crouching at the door; and its desire is for you, but you must master it* (**Genesis 4:6-7**).

Notice that God asks Cain three questions, all of which circle around what is in Cain's heart. God wants to have dialogue with Cain about what is bothering him so intensely, and He attempts to help Cain get to a more constructive and healthier place in his thoughts. God is trying to prevent a royal screwup by asking Cain to sit with what is in his heart and talk about this with God. But Cain never answered God's questions. That is problematic. Cain did not dialogue with God on what was bothering him, so the issues were not resolved constructively.

Have you ever had something troubling in your soul that became worse over time? Each of us has experienced some major difficulties in life that could include employment disasters, marital meltdowns, emotional earthquakes, financial catastrophes, relationship debacles, and heaps of other major struggles. I suggest that it is possible we could avoid such major catastrophes if we would step into the difficult conversations with God earlier in the timeline, perhaps dialoguing with God before the critical mass meltdown. I think His questions to Cain are also relevant to us today.

"Why are you angry? Why has your countenance fallen? Why are you upset?"

Instead of giving God the silent treatment and not answering His questions—as Cain did—I would propose that it is more constructive and healthier to actually engage in these difficult conversations with God. Maybe such a conversation would include something like:

- "God, I'm angry because You put me in a dysfunctional home."
- "God, I'm upset because I didn't get the promotion I wanted at work."
- "God, I'm majorly disappointed because my marriage hasn't turned out the way I thought it would."

These kinds of conversations require us to be honest with both ourselves and God. Let's appreciate that honesty is an essential ingredient for any intimate relationship, and it is vital for a constructive conversation.

But alas, Cain let the wound in his soul fester and grow to such intensity that he killed his brother when they were in the field together. He didn't dialogue with God before he murdered his brother despite God's attempt to engage and sit with Cain in his frustration and anger. Cain, therefore, royally screwed up.

And what happens when we royally screw up? God still endeavors to dialogue with us. In Genesis 4:9-15, we see the dialogue between God and Cain. That dialogue begins with, *"Where is Abel your brother?" And he said, "I do not know. Am I my brother's keeper?"* (Genesis 4:9).

Similar to God's question to Adam, God asks Cain where his brother is, even though He knows exactly what has transpired. Again, we see God endeavoring to draw Cain into a dialogue. Cain continues to resist the conversation by being deceptive, coy, and dismissive.

I am always sad when I read about Cain because I think there could have been several different and better outcomes to this story. I think Cain could have talked with God at the outset and expressed his frustration and disappointment, and I think Cain could have been forthcoming and told God that he had killed his brother.

Cain chose not to dialogue with God, and he chose to remain angry. This resulted in him killing his brother. And Cain was deceptive with God and did not repent from his destructive decision. Consequently, his decisions separated him from God. Cain lived the rest of his days wandering the earth instead of cultivating it, as he had done before.

As we finish this portion of the chapter, it is helpful to think about some lessons we can apply from the conversations that Adam and Cain had with God, particularly when we royally screw up with Him.

QUESTIONS FOR REFLECTION

1. Similar to Adam and Eve, are you afraid of God?

2. Where are the places in your life that you might be hiding from God?

3. Similar to Cain being disappointed that his vegetation offering was not well received, when are you disappointed with God? When do you not get the attention from God that you want, and are you willing to ask "why"?

4 Are you willing to let God help you grow?

CONVERSATION STARTER: EXAMEN

When we screw up, having a conversation with God can be problematic. We can have a wide array of feelings that make a conversation very difficult, such as feeling guilty, condemned, unworthy, afraid, anxious, inadequate, soiled, uncomfortable, and even numb. Maybe similar to Adam we try to hide from God, or like Cain we don't step into dialogue with God.

In an effort to start a conversation with God when you have screwed up royally, I would like to propose a daily exercise or platform for talking with God. This exercise comes from the Jesuit or Ignatian tradition, and it is called the *Examen*.

I appreciate that the name does not sound very appealing, particularly when we have really messed up; nevertheless, the name is the shortened form of the formal Ignatian practice, "Examination of Conscious." The purpose is to train us to recognize God in our daily living, regardless of how much we mess up or the severity of our failures.

Before I describe the steps for the Examen, it is helpful to remember some basic things about who God is from the conversations He had with Adam and Cain. Remember that God initiated conversations with Adam and Cain both before and after they screwed up. Their disobedience did not diminish God's faithfulness to them. Furthermore, God's conversations with these men were from a relational position and not a position of condemnation. Maybe it is helpful to remember that because God is triune—Father, Son, and Holy Spirit—this means that God is inherently relational by His sheer identity. And probably more important than anything is to remember what God's Word says in John 3:16-17:

> *For God so loved the world, that He gave His only begotten Son, that whoever believes in Him shall not perish, but have eternal life. For God did not send the Son into the world to judge the world, but that the world might be saved through Him.*

No matter what you have done, God loves you. That love does not change, because God is love and is unchanging. When you begin this Conversation Starter, it will be helpful to remember that God wants to connect with you regardless of what you have or haven't done. Let's get started!

The Examen is a conversation with God that endeavors to recognize God's presence and participation in our daily lives. To help accomplish this goal, there are five simple steps that can help us converse with God and recognize His presence. You could do these steps in the morning before you leave your home, or you could do them in the middle of the day, possibly over your lunch break. You could also do them at the end of the day before you lay down to sleep for the night.

There is lots of flexibility to this Conversation Starter, and you might find it helpful to experiment with some different times or methods for these steps. For example, you can do these steps by writing in a journal. You could make a note-card for each step and carry them with you to work through during your morning or evening commute. You could find a comfortable chair in your home and say each step aloud. Play around with what environment, timing, or techniques best facilitate conversing with God.

Perhaps what is most important with this exercise is not merely following each step, but also giving space and time at the end of each step for God's participation in this process. When you give God some room for input, it is possible that you will hear some words from God in your heart. It is also possible that you might feel some comfort, warmth, strength, loving-kindness, or grace. Maybe you will have a sense of cozy peace washing over you.

At some point in this journey, you might also sense God correcting you. Or you could also feel God giving you wisdom, encouragement, or direction. Maybe it would be helpful to keep notes on your phone or in a notebook about what you sense from God for each day with this Conversation Starter.

The following are the steps, along with some explanation, to help you apply this as your daily routine.[1]

1. Gratitude

In this step, you take an inventory of things that happened during the previous day for which you are grateful. You could start this conversation by saying something like, "God, thank You very much for helping me with the dicey conversation at work. Thank You for helping me get out the door on time. Thank You for helping me to be gracious rather than impatient with my spouse when [he or she] came home from work. Thank You for the creative solution with my schedule when I accidentally double-booked myself. Thank You for helping me cook dinner even when I was tired and didn't feel like it. Thank You for giving me wisdom to answer the hostile email from an in-law. Thank You for helping me pay my bills this month."

I sincerely *love* listing out all the things that happened in the previous day for which I am thankful! It is very energizing, and it gives me hope that God will participate in my current day. It also helps align my perspective to watch for God's participation in my real-time living. Being thankful is a good way to start a conversation with God: *"Enter His gates with thanksgiving and His courts with praise. Give thanks to Him, bless His name"* (Psalm 100:4).

2. Review

In this step, you will look over the preceding day—or a recent increment of time—and make note of when you sensed, heard, or noticed God. This is kind of like watching the recent day play on a movie screen in your imagination and looking for the places, experiences, or events where you notice God being involved. For example, as you think back over the day, maybe you received a text message from someone who was really encouraging and unexpected. Or maybe you had a conversation with someone, and something said resonated with your heart or had an impact on your soul. Perhaps you felt God with you in the car during rush-hour traffic, and God's presence made the commute more bearable or even enjoyable.

Doing this review gives God room to teach you how to pay attention to His participation in your daily living. Since we know that God is ever-present, we would be wise to let God coach and train us to recognize His presence! Again, you could write these observations in a notebook or journal, or you could just take mental notes of these God moments as you reflect on the recent time.

3. Sorrow

After going back through the previous day and looking for God, it is also helpful to look back and sense when you could have caused some pain or sorrow to God. What could have been some of your actions, words, decisions, behaviors, or attitudes for which you are remorseful? Did you say some sharp or hurtful words to your mate? Were you snarky or impatient with the bus driver or a fellow commuter? Did you post something cutting or sarcastic on someone's

Facebook wall? Did you say something that made politics more important than relationships?

As you look back over the previous day or brief span of time, it is important to consider our actions, words, attitudes, and decisions that could be displeasing to God. In this step, we invite Holy Spirit to convict us of behaviors that we might normally justify or ignore. This should be an important part of our conversation with God, particularly if we intend to grow closer to Him. This step has the potential to help us avoid a major screwup in the future by giving Holy Spirit the opportunity to help us with conviction in our daily living. It can help us recognize immediately when we have messed up, rather than letting stuff bloom into major issues.

4. Forgiveness

In this step, after you have identified the actions or situations in which you have caused pain, it is appropriate to ask for God's forgiveness. This process happens not only in the broad strokes and generalities, but also for the specific actions, words, decisions, attitudes, and thoughts that were displeasing to God.

It is one thing to feel sorrow in your heart for something, but when you speak out to God exactly what you did wrong and ask for forgiveness, it facilitates another level of intimacy. When we ask for forgiveness, we can be confident that we receive it: *"If we confess our sins, He is faithful and righteous to forgive us our sins and to cleanse us from all unrighteousness"* (1 John 1:9). Receiving forgiveness is a powerful experience that can help us grow in our connection with God.

The experiences I have had with my friends, kids, and husband prove this true for me. I'll never forget several years ago when I came to understand that my snarky comments to my husband were disrespectful and cutting. He was gracious for a long time, but suddenly it dawned on me how hurtful I had been to him with my disrespectful comments. When the light turned on for me with this revelation, I went to my husband and apologized sincerely for my disrespect. I then made a conscientious effort to honor him better. He forgave me graciously, and his forgiveness was a helpful ingredient in our marriage.

If this is true with our human relationships, how much more does God's forgiveness facilitate connection and intimacy with Him? In this part of your conversation with God, I would encourage you to pause to give yourself the opportunity to hear and experience God's forgiveness in your life— not only for the possible recent events, but also for the big struggles with which you might be wrestling.

5. Grace

In the final step for this conversation, it is helpful to ask both for God's grace that you will need for the next day and the ability to see God's presence more clearly. I really love this step because it faces forward and helps us look with hope to the future. Many people focus on and get stuck in the quagmire of the past. Asking for God's grace for the next day and asking for His help to be able to sense His presence are other ways to express Paul's words:

> *Brethren, I do not regard myself as having laid hold of it yet; but one thing I do: forgetting what lies behind and **reaching forward** to what lies ahead, I press on toward the goal for the prize of the upward call of God in Christ Jesus* (Philippians 3:13-14).

In this step of your conversation with God, let yourself be available and present with God's grace. His grace is powerful, transformational, and present every day with us. Each day is filled with God's fingerprints of grace that are ready and available for our discovery. I encourage you to ask God to prepare you to see and experience His grace in the upcoming hours or during the next day, without letting your focal point get too far into the future.

I have found the Jesuit Examen to be a very helpful Conversation Starter in my daily journey with God. I have used the whole Examen for extended periods of time, and I have used pieces of the Examen throughout my daily routines and in conversations with God. I can appreciate that for some people the Examen might be too regimented, or it could feel possibly heavily religious or legalistic. But perhaps a helpful perspective to the Examen is to think of it in simple and conversational terms, thereby ridding it of religious rigor and legalistic bondage. Try it on for size and give it an honest go with some time and purposeful engagement. You might be pleasantly surprised at the adventure that God has waiting for you.

For further reflection and note-taking see "Examen" on page 226 in the Epilogue.

ENDNOTE

1. James Martin, *The Jesuit Guide to Almost Everything* (New York: HarperCollins, 2010), 92-97.

3

CAN WE TALK—
SO WE CAN
BE CLOSER

Have you ever met someone who seemed to have such a deep walk with God that you were both mesmerized and just a little bit jealous? As I think back over the years, there are various people who stand out in my memory because of their walk with God. They inspired and challenged me to cultivate depth with God.

1. Malcolm Smith who taught the Bible out of a great depth and passion for being connected with God.

2. David Skinner who was a camp counselor at Omega Ranch during a summer camp. David had a sensitivity to Holy Spirit that I had never before seen demonstrated in daily living.

3. R. T. Kendall had depth with God through his knowledge of the New Testament and his expertise

in Greek scholarship, both of which I had never seen before.

4. Brother Mak had a special depth with God. It motivated him to live in China where he trusted God entirely and fed on God's faithfulness, guidance, protection, and effectiveness.

5. Richard Foster, who wrote *Celebration of Discipline,* helped me cultivate a deep intimacy with God that has sustained me through many fluctuating seasons of life.

These people, along with many others, have motivated me to develop a deeper walk with God, because I was able to see and feel their connection with Him. There have been numerous occasions when I walked away from conversations with these men having been provoked to strive for a deeper walk with God. The contrast between what I saw in my relationship with God and what I saw in their relationships with Him showed me that I could have more intimacy with Him. I asked them what their journey and their processes were that landed them with such a close connection with God. I saw the fruit, but I wanted to know how they got to such a place of intimacy.

In a similar way, I look at Abraham's intimacy with God and it provokes me. What did Abraham's very deep, fulfilling, effective, and connected walk with God look like? I believe that if we ask this question, it can help us frame our goal and describe the outcome that we are pursuing.

I think Abraham had one of the closest walks with God. The Bible says three times that Abraham was God's friend:

Second Chronicles 20:7; Isaiah 41:8; and James 2:23. If God considered Abraham to be His friend, what did that look like? After we consider what it looked like, then we will look at aspects of the journey Abraham walked so that we can integrate some steps to help us cultivate a deeper walk with God. We will also look at conversations between the two of them, making some poignant observations that we can fold into our daily living.

What did Abraham's deeply intimate and richly connected friendship with God look like? The best place to see this relationship in action can be found in Genesis 18. This chapter is very compelling, particularly in light of the conversation that transpires between God and Abraham. This conversation starts when God shows up at the door to Abraham's tent, and Abraham invites Him to stay for a meal.

The idea of God coming to my house for dinner is at the same time disturbing and appealing! I would be disturbed to have God come over for dinner for lots of reasons. For starters, my house is often very messy because I am not a good housekeeper. I have three teenage kids, and my family does not live on the tidy and neat end of the *Better Homes and Gardens* spectrum. It is not uncommon for there to be dishes in the sink, Tupperware on the counter, socks by the sofa, and dust bunnies in the corners, to say nothing of the junk mail accumulating on the kitchen counter.

I would also be jittery about having God come over for dinner because sometimes my cooking can go off the rails. Here is an insider secret: in my home, we measure the tastiness of a meal that I cook by the number of smoke alarms that go off in the house while I'm cooking. The more smoke alarms, the tastier the meal will be!

In contrast, on the appealing side of having God come over for dinner, I would be massively excited to sit down with Him and share not only a good dinner, but even better, some rich conversation and deep quality time. I can only imagine how the conversation would go, probably with lots of laughter, wisdom, grace, encouragement, truth, insight, and connectedness. To get to spend a big chunk of time with God sitting at my kitchen table and sharing a meal together is very appealing—even if my house is messy!

INTIMACY BEGETS...

Intimacy Begets Access

In a similar fashion, when God showed up at the door of Abraham's tent, Abraham was very excited to make a meal for God, to spend time in conversation, and to cultivate an even stronger, connected relationship. Abraham's intimacy with God, which he had been faithful to cultivate for many years, was instrumental in God coming to have dinner with Abraham. And when God showed up for dinner, Abraham and Sarah went to great lengths to lay down a feast for Him (see Genesis 18:6-8). They prepared to have some wonderful connection time. The feast would facilitate both conversation, vulnerability, participation, and connection.

Intimacy Begets Vulnerability

At the end of the meal, God brought up a very sensitive and dicey subject with Abraham—Sarah's infertility. God spoke with Abraham about how Sarah was going to become pregnant within the next year, even though she was past the childbearing years and was in disbelief. This was a tender subject for Sarah and Abraham, because of the cultural and historical value placed on women and their ability to produce children at this time. Sarah, who was barren, had even offered her maidservant, Hagar, to Abraham to have children (see Genesis 16).

Despite Sarah's best efforts and resourceful scheming, she was not able to give Abraham a child. This caused friction and angst in their marriage (see Genesis 16:4-5). God stepped into this tender subject when He told Abraham that Sarah would get pregnant and bear a child in the next year.

I find this conversation between God and Abraham intriguing and appealing, because the willingness to discuss a vulnerable topic reveals an intimacy that God had with Abraham. The conversation between Abraham and God reminds me of some dinner discussions that we have had with some close friends, the Johnsons. These are God-given friends to my husband and me. We regularly enjoy meals at each other's houses with some really great conversations. Most of the time, there is lots of laughter and good-hearted ribbing. And there are also times when we are very vulnerable with each other about tender subjects such as our kids, health challenges, God's direction in our lives, personal struggles, and lots more.

When we are close to people, we can be vulnerable and have conversations with them about sensitive subjects, similar to God talking with Abraham about Sarah getting pregnant in the next year.

Intimacy Begets Participation

Not only did God and Abraham converse about the tender subject of Sarah's upcoming pregnancy, God also talked with Abraham about His concerns and possible plans for Sodom and Gomorrah: *"The Lord said, 'Shall I hide from Abraham what I am about to do'"* (Genesis 18:17). This is the beginning of the conversation God has with Abraham about the future of Sodom and Gomorrah. In this conversation, Abraham dared to challenge God about His decision for these cities based on His character.

Consider Abraham's words in Genesis 18:24-25:

> *Suppose there are fifty righteous within the city; will You indeed sweep it away and not spare the place for the sake of the fifty righteous who are in it? Far be it from You to do such a thing, to slay the righteous with the wicked, so that the righteous and the wicked are treated alike. Far be it from You! Shall not the Judge of all the earth deal justly?*

This conversation about Sodom and Gomorrah continues with Abraham pressing God to answer his challenge with fewer and fewer numbers of righteous people in these cities. Ultimately, the conversation with God concludes with Abraham asking God not to destroy Sodom and Gomorrah if there are ten righteous people to be found in these cities. God agrees to Abraham's request (see Genesis 18:32).

Let's take a moment to appreciate that Abraham had such an intimate and deep relationship with God that he could intercede with Him on behalf of some very wicked cities. This conversation between Abraham and God is very unique in the Old Testament, and it shows a particularly intimate relationship between God and Abraham. But this level of intimacy did not come out of nowhere. There is a backstory to explore and learn from so that we can also grow in our intimacy with God.

So how did Abraham grow into such a deep relationship with God? What did their conversations entail that could facilitate such a close connection? If we want to have deep and intimate conversations with God, what would the incremental steps look like at the beginning of the relationship? Thankfully, we can read about the growing intimacy that Abraham had with God through some very interesting conversations in Genesis 15 and 17. In these chapters, we see that Abraham made decisions to grow closer with God by his conversations and actions.

This reminds me about the intentionality of cultivating a deepening friendship with our dinner couple, the Johnsons. We happened to meet the Johnsons during a family vacation on a cruise ship. At this time, I was under a writing deadline, so I wasn't able to spend much time with them. However, we were able to join them for some dinners. When we returned to Denver, we agreed to continue to grow our friendship.

From this decision, we have developed a really vibrant friendship. Over the course of several years, we have shared vulnerable needs, enjoyed meals, laughed a boatload, and enjoyed great fellowship together. Through many transitions in life, we have prayed for each other, been supportive and encouraging, and have provided helpful wisdom and a safe sounding board for each other. None of this happens without being purposeful.

Such purposeful engaging is what God does with Abram in Genesis 15 when He speaks with him about gathering together several animals. God's conversation with Abram is expressed through the covenant activities described in this chapter, and they are all initiated by God. Abram responds by collecting the animals that God specifies, slicing them in half and protecting them from birds of prey. As the day wears on, Abram falls into a deep sleep and has a dream where he sees a smoking oven and flaming torch going between the animal halves. In this dream, God makes a covenant with him in which He promises Abram both the land where he was living and future offspring.

It is noteworthy to me that all of this happened because of God's initiative. We must realize that God is initiating a deepening relationship with us—not the other way around. We are responding to God's continual initiatives. He is beckoning us to experience His loving-kindness. He gives us grace, wisdom, and strength, invites us to a deeper relationship with Him, enters our daily living for fellowship, and connects with us! It would be helpful to take a few moments to think about the various ways and experiences in which God has initiated a connection and relationship with us.

While it can be helpful to see the different ways God has initiated various conversations and activities with us—directing our lives, intervening in different circumstances, and coordinating supernatural "coincidences"—we would also be wise to look at the proper ways to respond to God. We can look at the conversation that transpired between God and Abram in Genesis 17. This happened well after the God-initiated covenant that was described in Genesis 15.

In the conversation that Abram had with God in Genesis 17, we see some interesting dialogue. To begin with, God shows up in Abram's life when Abram is ninety-nine years old. Right away, He talks with Abram—for sixteen verses. In these verses, God uses the word "covenant" nine times. This is significant because it demonstrates the importance that God places on His relationship and commitment with Abram. In Old Testament times, covenant was the highest and most intense form of relational connection and commitment with someone outside of marriage, which was its own covenant relationship. By establishing a covenant relationship with Abram, God is committing Himself to staying connected with him.

I also suggest that commitment is an essential ingredient for cultivating a deep and connected relationship. I see this to be true in our friendship with the Johnsons. We are mutually committed to this friendship, which is expressed by our consistency. We are all very intentional about getting together on a regular basis regardless of the demands of life or our busy schedules. There is always a reason to be busy or not to connect, so it is all the more important that we are purposeful about staying connected!

The same holds true for God with Abram. Not only does God emphasize covenant and commitment in these verses, He also changes Abram's name to Abraham to match the future that God has for Abraham. This change denotes the fruitfulness that will characterize Abraham's growing family. It is again noteworthy to consider that as Abraham's intimacy and connection with God grow, his name and identity change. To be sure, the closer the relationship we have with God, the more our identity can change to become more closely aligned with our divine design!

Up to this point, God's communication with Abraham has been very positive—an improvement in Abraham's name, God confirming a covenant with Abraham, and God expressing His commitment to Abraham's family and future nation. On the heels of such positive input, God tells Abraham that he is required to circumcise all the males in his household. In this directive, God is communicating to Abraham that he is a participant in this relationship, not merely a spectator or a recipient. True intimacy requires participation and engagement with both parties involved in the relationship. Intimacy and connection are not sustained, nor do they grow, if both participants do not contribute to the relationship.

This principle also holds true in our friendship with the Johnsons. Both couples recognize the importance and necessity of contributing and participating toward that relationship. It is not so much about the quantity or intensity of the contribution or participation as much as it is about demonstrating the commitment to maintaining a growing and vibrant friendship.

Once God communicates with Abraham about His covenant, changes Abraham's name, and reveals the circumcision requirement, Abraham makes an internal reply and an external expression: *"Then Abraham fell on his face and laughed, and said in his heart, 'Will a child be born to a man one hundred years old? And will Sarah, who is ninety years old, bear a child?'"* (Genesis 17:17).

I love this verse because it shows how we often react in conversations with God. When I think back to different conversations I have had with Him, I have often said something to God that was different from what I actually believed in my heart. I suspect that could be true for you as well. We often know what we are supposed to say, the right words, religious platitudes, and answers we think we should give, and yet end up saying and doing the opposite.

Despite possibly knowing the proper religious etiquette with God, Abraham was honest and fell on his face and laughed. Sometimes the stuff that God says to us can seem really far-fetched. Sometimes we struggle to believe that God's promises are real and powerful, and sometimes we find it challenging to agree that God is even better than what we think about Him on a sunny day. Sometimes there is an internal conflict in what we think versus what we hear from God. And to this end, I am grateful that Abraham was honest about this internal struggle.

Furthermore, I appreciate that Abraham attempted to help God resolve the infertility challenge with Sarah, his wife, by proposing that Ishmael could be his offspring (see Genesis 17:18). But God does not need our help, as we can see from God's reply to Abraham. God continues the conversation with Abraham by making it clear that Sarah will bear a son to Abraham within the next year, despite her age and the seeming impossibility (see Genesis 17:20-21).

In this conversation, we see the back and forth nature between God and Abraham as they discuss not only God's promise to Abraham, but also Abraham's willingness to change and agree with God's plans. We also see in this conversation a reflection of our own humanity in the way that Abraham replies to God. He starts with incredulity and then offers possible solutions to an impossible situation. I am very grateful to have the dialogue between God and Abraham documented, because it permits me to step into some similar conversations with God about various impossibilities, the future, and God's plans!

As we finish this chapter, we can see the incremental progress in Abraham's intimacy with God. This process begins in Genesis 15 with the covenant activities that Abram does, continues into Genesis 17 and the covenant conversation with God, and culminates in Genesis 18 with an incredible dinner and subsequent conversation with God. If the relationship with our friends, the Johnsons, can be so rich and deep, how much more connected and intimate can we be with God? This can take place through vulnerable dialogue, committed connection, and adventurous faith. Let's stay on God's page and remain committed to a vibrant and growing intimacy with Him!

QUESTIONS FOR REFLECTION

1. Look back on your life and take an inventory of where you have seen God working and moving. Were these events initiated by you or by God? How would you respond to these events today?

2. In what ways do you see your current identity misaligned with the identity God has given you? In what ways could you see God wanting to change and reshape your identity to match His design?

3. Based on Abraham's conversations with God, what are some actions and decisions you could make to deepen your relationship with God?

4. What is an incremental step you could take to be more committed to your relationship with God?

CONVERSATION STARTER:
PRAYING WITH HOLY SPIRIT

When I look at the overview of Abraham's life, I am very intrigued by the increasingly close relationship he had with God—even being identified as God's friend (see Isaiah 41:8 and James 2:23). In this Conversation Starter, we look at a method you can use to cultivate a deeper relationship with God with the aim of becoming intimate friends. I am introducing you to this Conversation Starter with great enthusiasm because of my own experience of having used it over the course of several years.

In my journey with God, my central and continuous goal is to grow increasingly intimate with Him. I have learned that Holy Spirit is essential for this deepening intimacy. Jesus told us that Holy Spirit would always be with us, *"I will ask the Father, and He will give you another Helper, that He may be with you forever"* (John 14:16). Since Holy Spirit is always with us, it makes sense to get to know Him. Holy Spirit is part of our triune God and is paramount to our ability to grow in intimacy and connection with God. To this end, I have written a few books about Holy Spirit that could help you grow in understanding who this wonderful Person is. The titles are *Heavenly Help* and *In Step with the Spirit*.

As I have grown closer to God through getting to know Holy Spirit better, I have found lots of experiences, practices, insights, and processes that have helped me cultivate a growing intimacy with God. One of my favorite discoveries for starting an intimate conversation with God has been a method based on the verbs associated with Holy Spirit in Romans 8. I discovered that this chapter has the most references to and descriptions of Holy Spirit in the entire Bible. There are almost twenty mentions of Holy Spirit in approximately twenty verses. Having made this discovery, I identified nine key actions with Holy Spirit for our daily living. As a Conversation Starter, almost every morning I take each verb and sit with Holy Spirit in that verb.

What I mean by "sit with Holy Spirit in a verb" is that I choose in sequence one of the Romans 8 verbs and either take time to let Holy Spirit speak to me, or I reflect on what He could to do with that verb in my life. I take time to pause and keep myself open to Holy Spirit's input around these verbs. I may not always hear words or get concrete input about a verb. Sometimes, what I sense is more of an impression, a feeling, a gentle suggestion, or a tender nudge that accompanies the verb I am attending to at that moment. The resulting conversations are rich, deep, illuminating, transformational, and stabilizing, leading me into ever-deepening intimacy with Holy Spirit. I want to introduce you to this Conversation Starter and walk you through what it could look like for you, as well as encourage you to explore this adventure with Holy Spirit for yourself. Let's jump in!

We will look at each verb in the order listed in Romans 8, because I find this order to be an ever-deepening journey and conversation with Holy Spirit. We will consider each verb in light of how it is used in that particular verse of Romans 8 to ensure that we are true to the biblical context. Additionally, after I list the verb, I give a brief description of the verb and suggest some ways to be present with Holy Spirit in that verb. At the end of this chapter, I present some ideas that could help you integrate this Conversation Starter into your daily routine.

The following is our Conversation Starter with Holy Spirit:

Walk: "*...who do not walk according to the flesh but according to the Spirit*" (Romans 8:4). This word *walk* in the Greek is *peripateo*, and it means to walk alongside or to walk around. When I start this conversation with Holy Spirit, I ask Him to walk alongside me over the course of the day. I then ask Him to help me be aware of His presence as He is walking alongside me. I also ask Holy Spirit to direct my steps.

I keep my to-do list handy so that I can write down whatever I hear, specifically helpful reminders for things I need to accomplish that day.

Think: *"...but the mind set on the Spirit is life and peace"* (Romans 8:6). This phrase *mind set* in Greek is *phroneo*, and it means the outlook or mindset. These words relate to our soul and include our thoughts, emotions, desires, perspectives, attention, and cognitive processes. As I continue the conversation with Holy Spirit, I ask for His input and help with everything related to my soul. With this verb, I invite Him to engage with and direct my emotions, thoughts, focus, desires, and perspective. I am keen to have Holy Spirit participate in the activities and processes of my soul.

Dwell: *"...if indeed the Spirit of God dwells in you"* (Romans 8:9). This word *dwell* is our English word for *oikeo* in the Greek. *Oikeo* means to live, to take up residence, and to dwell. This word circles around the ideas of family, home, residence, and house. When I bring this word into my conversation with Holy Spirit, I invite Him to live in me, to take up residence, and to make Himself at home throughout all of me. During this part of the conversation, I pause to ask what places within my heart I might be withholding from Him. I also invite Holy Spirit to dwell in every area of my life—marriage, kids, community, work, travels, hobbies, friendships, values, decisions, etc. I find the word *dwell* to be a very intimate word, because home is where I let down my hair, relax, exhale, get comfortable, and just be. When I invite Holy Spirit to dwell in me, I am giving Him permission to settle into the core of me and to live at home in me.

Make alive: *"...will also give life to your mortal bodies through His Spirit who dwells in you"* (Romans 8:11). This is an interesting verb in the Greek, *zoepoieo*. It is interesting, because it references the resurrection or making alive of Jesus in correlation with Holy Spirit making us alive. When I first conversed with Holy Spirit about this action or verb, I was perplexed. I already considered myself to be alive and not dead. But in our conversation, I felt Him talking with me about places in my life that are dead, nonresponsive, or dormant. And at a deeper level, even now when I participate in this conversation, I sense Holy Spirit dealing with me about my divine blueprint. He talks to me about who God has made me and how some of that divine design has been injured, or made comatose because of various life circumstances, experiences, satan's efforts, human interactions, and traumas. In this part of the conversation, I bring these memories, experiences, etc., to Holy Spirit to renovate and make alive. Indeed, I want to live fully from the blueprint that God has designed in me!

Put to death: *"...by the Spirit you are putting to death the deeds of the body..."* (Romans 8:13). This word in the Greek, *thanatoo*, has zero appeal for me. I don't like death, and everything associated with death is a hard pass for me. So, this part of the conversation with Holy Spirit has been tricky for me. I would like to ignore it altogether. But when I sit with Holy Spirit in this verb, to put to death, it causes me to pause and consider what in my life needs to die. These areas could include destructive habits or routines, distorted perspectives or outlooks, unhealthy conversations, deceptive mindsets, or identities that are not aligned with my divine design. When

I converse with Holy Spirit on this verb, I invite Him to look into me and show me what needs to be put to death. This includes stuff like deception, unforgiveness, and whatever is contrary to genuine love in my life.

Being led: "...*being led by the Spirit of God, these are sons of God*" (Romans 8:14). The word *led* in the Greek is *ago,* and it means to carry, lead, bring, or guide. The key catalyst in this part of the conversation for being led or guided by Holy Spirit relates to being a son or daughter of God. When I come to this verb in my conversation with Holy Spirit, I acknowledge that I am God's daughter; therefore, I can be directed or led by Him. This is noteworthy, because we can sometimes find ourselves following after our earthly parents in our perspectives, our values, possible job alignment, relational patterns, or maybe some destructive behaviors. This verb, *ago*, is a massive necessity for aligning our identity as God's child, and then following Holy Spirit from that alignment.

Testify: "*The Spirit Himself testifies with our spirit that we are children of God*" (Romans 8:16). This is a critical verb for us to consider as we grow in our conversation with God, because it speaks to the core of who we are by divine creation and purpose. In the Greek, this is the verb *summartureo*, and it is the compound word *sum-martureo*. Here's the big deal: at this point in the conversation with Holy Spirit, our true self is discovered and lived only with His help and participation. The Greek word *summartureo* literally means together witness or testify. What is Holy Spirit giving witness of or testimony to in our lives? Holy Spirit testifies with our core self—our spirit or interior identity—that we are God's son or daughter—our divine design. I welcome Him to participate and speak deeply to me to remind me that I am not a spectator or outsider in God's family. I am an integral part of this family. I encourage you to sit with this verb in your own conversation with Holy Spirit to let it become alive and to resonate in your core identity!

Help: *"...Spirit also helps our weakness..."* (Romans 8:26). Do you need help? The honest truth is that you and I need help because we have weaknesses. Your weaknesses could be different from mine, but that fact doesn't mean I need more or less help than you. I might just need different help. It is very appealing to me that in my conversation with Holy Spirit I can ask for help, since this is one of the verbs associated with Holy Spirit in Romans 8.

The word *help* in Greek is *sunantilambanomai*. It is used only one other time in Scripture. You will find this word used in Luke 10:40 when Martha asked Jesus to make Mary, her sister, *help* her. In this part of the conversation, I invite Holy Spirit to join me and help me in my weaknesses. This includes not only the weaknesses of which I am aware, but also the weaknesses of which I am not aware—the blind spots. The more I talk about getting help from Holy Spirit, the more comfortable I become with the idea. I now relish and delight in Him helping me! In this part of the conversation, you might consider looking at your weaknesses and writing them down. You can then invite Holy Spirit to help specifically with each weakness, taking an occasional pause to see if He would add some new weak spots that might have escaped your awareness.

Intercede: *"...but the Spirit Himself intercedes for us..."* (Romans 8:26). When I come to this final verb in my conversation with Holy Spirit, it never ceases to astound me that He would speak and intervene on my behalf! This verb is *hyperentugxano* in the Greek. It is only used this one time in the New Testament, and it conveys the idea of Holy Spirit praying for us. It is a powerful picture of Holy Spirit standing in the middle interceding for us in very deep and profound ways. With this verb, I invite Him to mediate or stand in the middle of difficult situations, conversations, potential challenges, struggles, and events where I am unsettled or inadequate.

As I finish this conversational journey with Holy Spirit, I am often very encouraged and deeply grounded in an overwhelming sense of peace and genuine love. I have found it abundantly helpful to converse with Holy Spirit through this journey on a daily basis, appreciating that I don't always have the time to do each verb. Even though I sometimes struggle to do all of the verbs, I am never disappointed when I do any part or piece of this conversation. There are many days when I will only have enough time to get through the *dwelling* part of the conversation, or possibly up to the part about *putting to death* the things in me that are not aligned with my divine destiny. No matter how much time I have or how far I make it in this conversational journey, it is almost always an amazing experience for me. I encourage you to have this conversational journey with Holy Spirit in your daily living. As you do so, fasten your seatbelt for the adventure of your life!

As a concluding thought, it is also helpful to consider the tenses for the verbs that I have just outlined. In the Greek language, a present tense verb means that the action is continuous and ongoing. This means that the action for these verbs does not have stopping or starting points, pauses, or conclusions. Keeping this in mind, consider that all of these verbs in Romans 8 are used in the present tense, with the exception of the verb *to make alive*, which is used in the future tense. When you participate with Holy Spirit in this conversation, remember that all of the action is for now. It is not just in the past when Paul wrote the book of Romans, and it is not just for some distant and elusive future that is not relevant for this day. Each day, these verbs can be relevant and conversational for you with Holy Spirit as you grow closer and more intimate with God.

The following are some suggestions for integrating these verbs into a daily routine:

- Journaling: You might find it helpful to each day take a page or so to write each verb and what Holy Spirit intends for you. You want to be purposeful with time and attention, but not mechanical or rote.

- Work commute: You could write out these verbs on an index card or make a note in your phone and speak them quietly to yourself, inviting Holy Spirit to converse with you about each one.

- Lunch break: Sometimes it is helpful to take a moment or two during your lunch break to look at these verbs and allow time for conversation with Holy Spirit.

- Bedtime: Before settling into bed, you might find it helpful to look purposefully at each verb, pausing to let Holy Spirit direct you.

As we finish with this Conversation Starter, I encourage you to receive Holy Spirit's invitation to join this journey for several months of daily discussion with these verbs. I think you will be pleasantly surprised, and maybe even astounded, with the adventure that waits for you with this conversation!

For further reflection and note-taking see "Praying With Holy Spirit" on page 228 in the Epilogue.

4

CAN WE TALK—
I'M AT A FORK IN THE ROAD

"You have to make quick decisions!"
This was the advice my friend gave me when I first tried to snowboard in the trees. Prior to this experience, I had only snowboarded wide, groomed, and smooth runs with no obstacles. Learning how to snowboard in the trees where the spaces are narrow, where there are logs submerged under the snow, and where tree branches stretch across any "path" is no easy challenge. It was all the more daunting to me because I was the beginner in the group. I was still getting proficient on my board, and I was stressed out that I was making everyone wait on me because I kept falling to avoid tree bashing.

Learning to snowboard in trees isn't just navigating a fork in the road. It is the avoidance of branches, steering around hidden obstacles, regulating one's speed for safe navigation, and possibly finding a path that others have forged—unless you're looking for fresh powder and the way less traveled.

I can appreciate that snowboarding around trees is a second-by-second experience when it comes to making decisions about the proverbial fork in the road. Life is all about navigating various forks in the road, such as choosing a college, making dating decisions, considering career options, deciding about marriage and children, and selecting a living location. What do we do with such major decisions? These kinds of choices can be far more daunting and stressful than just the quick left or right turn to avoid a tree while snowboarding!

When I think about steering through various significant choices, I often find myself looking at Jacob, the son of Isaac and grandson of Abraham. We read about his life in Genesis chapters 25–35, 37, and 42–50. As we read through these chapters, we see that Jacob came to three major forks in the road. Of course, he had lots of daily decisions that were important, one of which was obeying his mom, Rebekah, to deceive his dad, Isaac. He also decided to trick his brother, Esau, to gain Esau's birthright. He made the decision to pursue Rachel as his wife, to live separately from Esau later in his life, and to send his sons to Egypt to buy food during a massive famine. Jacob is a lot like us when it comes to making important decisions throughout our lives. But what did Jacob do when he faced major forks in the road?

JACOB AT BETHEL

I suggest that the first major fork in the road in Jacob's life occurred when Esau threatened to kill him, and he ran from Esau. Jacob chose to leave his home, family, comfort, and everything he knew to go to a place he had never been. This could be a bit like the decisions we face when we are finishing high school and trying to figure out where to go and what to do next; however, for Jacob, he had to meet new people and carve out his own life without the safety net of being able to return home if catastrophe struck.

In my own life, this season of becoming an adult had lots of forks in the road. I had decided to go to college at Oral Roberts University when I was in high school, but during my college years I made lots of decisions about what I would study, who I would date, what I would believe, who would be some lifelong friends, and what kind of degree or profession I would pursue. I remember the pressure I felt when trying to decide what I would choose as my major. I'll never forget telling one of my friends, "It is ludicrous to think an eighteen-year-old will be able to make a decision about what major to select that will guide the rest of her life!" I could barely think about my next assignment due in college, let alone make a decision for a possible career I would have to live with for the rest of my life.

Leading up to Jacob's fork in the road, he had just lied to his dad by pretending to be Esau, his brother. Because of this deception, Isaac thought he was blessing Esau. In reality, though, he was blessing Jacob, the younger of these twin sons. When Esau learned that Jacob had stolen the blessing from their dad by his deception, he was enraged and threatened to kill Jacob. In response, Rebekah, their mom, stepped in to protect her son. She suggested that Jacob move far away to her brother's household.

Jacob ran for his life. On his journey to his uncle's house, he had a very supernatural dream in a place called Bethel where God met him and gave him some very specific promises. God told Jacob that He would be with him during his sojourn, He would multiply his family, give him the land he was sleeping on, protect him, and bring him back to this homeland (see Genesis 28:13-15). I have no doubt that at this fork in the road, Jacob was very comforted by this supernatural experience and these promises, particularly since he had no idea what was in his immediate future.

In this conversation with God, it is interesting to consider what Jacob replied: *"Then Jacob awoke from his sleep and said, 'Surely the Lord is in this place, and I did not know it'"* (Genesis 28:16).

While there is not a lot of dialogue in this conversation between God and Jacob, a very important truth is established for Jacob in this experience. He learned that God is with him whether he realized it or not. And this important truth applies to us as well. It reveals to us that we can have a conversation with God at any time because He is always with us whether or not we are aware of it.

I love this truth because it opens up the possibility that I can have a conversation with God anytime, anywhere, in any circumstance or situation. Indeed, it is even possible to have an ongoing dialogue or experience with God even when I sleep! Jacob learned this truth during his first major fork in the road, at Bethel.

JACOB AT PENIEL AND MAHANAIM

At Jacob's second major fork in the road, he had a massively significant conversation with God that changed not only his mobility, but also his perspective and identity (see Genesis 32). In order to appreciate the gravity of this conversation, we have to consider the backstory that led to this experience. Prior to this fork in the road, Jacob had worked for his uncle, Laban, for twenty years. He had been tricked by Laban into marrying Laban's less-than-pretty daughter, Leah, after working for Laban for seven years.

When Jacob agreed to work another seven years for Laban, he was given Laban's beautiful daughter, Rachel, as his wife. Furthermore, Jacob received wages for working for his uncle in the form of sheep, goats, and cattle; therefore, with God's blessing, Jacob was extremely prosperous.

In Genesis 31:1-16, this second fork in the road of Jacob's life becomes evident. These verses describe how Laban's sons were jealous of Jacob's growing prosperity, how God spoke to Jacob about going back to his homeland, and how his wives agreed with Jacob about moving away from their father and returning to his homeland.

These verses reveal three important factors we should consider when pursuing God's input about making major decisions in our lives:

1. Consider God's Word. What does the Bible say about a decision you might be making? Is there biblical alignment for one path more than another? It is important that we make decisions that are aligned with biblical principles.

2. What do you sense in your heart? In Genesis 31:3, God spoke to Jacob and told him to return to his homeland.

3. Circumstantial agreement is important. In Genesis 31:1-16, it is clear that the circumstances supported what Jacob was sensing in his heart. The welcome Jacob had experienced with Laban had evaporated. Laban's sons were jealous of Jacob's prosperity, and Jacob's wives were in agreement about returning to Jacob's homeland.

In this last point about circumstantial agreement, I recognize that circumstances cannot always lead or control the decisions we make. Sometimes our circumstances seem to be opposed to what we sense God is saying to us in our hearts. When this happens, it is wise to pause, take inventory, and consider the timing for our decisions and actions.

Let's also be certain that just because God leads us in a particular direction does not mean that this direction will be smoothy groovy. For example, when I was first learning to snowboard, I was following a friend who had been snow-boarding for several years. She was really good. As I followed her, she led me to a run that was filled with moguls. Moguls are bumps in the snow that can range from ankle or shin height all the way to thigh or hip high, and they usually fill parts of a ski run. They can make the hillside look like undulating terrain. For experts, this can be a fun challenge. For beginners, like myself at that time, this kind of terrain looks like a page from Dante's *Inferno*.

As I followed my friend into this nightmare, the two tips of my board got lodged on the tops of two moguls. I was stuck in the middle of my board, bouncing up and down, trying to figure out how to get dislodged without getting injured. Ultimately, my friend helped me get through all of the land-mine moguls by telling me to stay on the side of the ski run where there weren't any moguls. I was to board on the edge of the run that dropped into a dense forest where I could easily tree bash and possibly be severely injured. Needless to say, this wasn't my favorite snowboarding experience. Sometimes, like learning to snowboard through moguls, it is bumpy when we follow God. But let's still follow God and keep up the conversation even when life is not very groovy.

As Jacob followed God through bumpy terrain, he came to a fork in the road that was really challenging. After he left Laban—taking his wives, all of his many children (eleven sons at this point), and abundant wealth—he had to face the reality that he was running into a situation from which he had fled twenty years earlier—Esau's death threat. Jacob was returning to his homeland and would have to meet Esau. He had a lot to lose. So much so that he sent all of his possessions and his family ahead across the Jordan River while he spent the night on the other side.

At this fork in the road at Peniel, Jacob experienced an all-night wrestling match with God (see Genesis 32:24-32). The conversation Jacob had with God during this situation is very significant for us. Sometimes it seems like we are in a wrestling match with God trying to figure out what is happening, where we are going, or why we are in this situation. Maybe we are trying to make sense of what has happened in the past or where God has been participating in our lives. Sometimes like Jacob, we wrestle with God.

Let's also look at Jacob's conversation with God at this fork in the road. God told Jacob to let go of Him; and even though Jacob's hip had been dislocated during the wrestling match, he told God that he would not let go unless God blessed him. God answered by asking Jacob's name. When Jacob replied, God changed Jacob's name (which means *deceiver*) to Israel (which means *one who wrestles with God*). After this renaming, Jacob asked for God's name. God asked why Jacob wanted to know His name, and then He blessed Jacob.

This conversation is interesting for lots of reasons. To begin with, let's appreciate that a conversation and wrestling match with God can change the way we walk, the way we do life, and how we move through the rest of our lives. Perhaps the limp that Jacob sustained from wrestling with God served to remind him for the rest of his life that God is sovereign. Let us always remember that God's ways and thoughts are higher than our ways and thoughts (see Isaiah 55:8-9).

Furthermore, our conversations with God have the potential to reframe our identity, similar to the way that God changed Jacob's name to Israel. We see this principle throughout the Bible. God changed the names of Abram to Abraham, Sarai to Sarah, and Simon to Peter. These shifts in name reflect a shift in identity. When we have an ongoing dialogue with God, we would be wise to let God change our identity to more closely align with how He has designed us and who He has made us to be.

Finally, let's place a platinum priority on walking with God and keeping Him in our life no matter what. In this conversation and wrestling match, Jacob wouldn't let go of God, no matter how tired he was, no matter the time of night, no matter his physical pain or weakness, and no matter what God said or did. Jacob did not let go of God. We also know that God never leaves or forsakes us. *"...the Lord your God is the one who goes with you. He will not fail you or forsake you"* (Deuteronomy 31:6). Let's be entirely committed that we will not leave Him.

JACOB AT BEERSHEBA

In the final conversation between God and Jacob/Israel, he was in his twilight years. It was at this time he learned that his son, Joseph, whom he thought was dead, was not only alive but was second in command in Egypt. In this conversation with God, found in Genesis 46:1-5, Jacob was leaving his homeland, where there was a raging famine, and was moving to Egypt where there was food, lodging, protection, and provision—all because of Joseph's leadership. It is noteworthy to consider that this conversation with God also happened at night, as did both his first conversation with God at Bethel and the all-night wrestling match at Peniel.

I bring up the reality of Jacob's night conversations with God because it can be helpful to realize that we can have some very powerful and transforming conversations with God when life is dark.

If you have ever awakened in the night and there is no clock nearby, the night can seem to move along slowly, with endless seconds. In the darkness, we can get discouraged by life's circumstances, uncertainty, unresolved struggles, provision gaps, and lots more. I think Jacob possibly felt the same at Bethel—unsure about his future and groping in the darkness of the challenges of his familial relationships. But God spoke to him at night in a dream, and this conversation gave Jacob hope in the morning. I suggest that the same was true for Jacob when he wrestled with God at Peniel before he crossed the Jordan river to meet his brother, Esau, whom he had not seen for twenty years—more uncertainty and unresolved family tension.

Here at Beersheba, Jacob/Israel has his third nighttime conversation with God. Once again, he has left a place where he had been comfortable for multiple decades to go somewhere he has never been. It seems to me that these nighttime conversations for Jacob served as dividing lines between a previous season and the beginning of a new season. Let's appreciate that in the dark seasons of life we can have some amazing conversations with God. These conversations can foster a new sunrise and a change in a particular season of life in which we find ourselves. A nighttime conversation with God can be massively transformational!

In addition to this conversation at night, let's consider that this fork in the road for Jacob came at a time in his life when he would have likely preferred not to experience major changes. At this fork in the road, Jacob was elderly, settled comfortably in the land God had promised him, surrounded by his family, and probably content with life—besides the pesky famine that was forcing him to make hard decisions. Indeed, he had to choose between moving to Egypt and helping his family survive with Joseph's assistance or staying in God's promised land and his family starving to death from the famine. Despite Jacob's age and probable desires to stay in what he knew to be comfortable and familiar, he chose to move his family to Egypt. God affirmed Jacob's decision in their nighttime conversation at Beersheba.

As a personal example of this, when I sustained a fairly severe concussion after a snowboarding accident, I had to face a fork in the road regarding my future with this hobby. On the day of the accident, I had been riding aggressively on a snowboard that wasn't very stable. During a particularly speedy run, I heard this little voice in my mind tell me that I should slow down, but I didn't. As I was flying down the mountain, I caught an edge with my snowboard, did a back flip, and smashed down on my head. I am pretty sure that I blacked out. When the fog began to clear, I was really shaken. I gingerly made my way down to the ski lift.

The recovery from this concussion seemed interminable, and I began to contemplate if I should continue to snowboard or if I should put my gear up for sale and retire. At this fork in the road, I realized that I immensely enjoyed this sport. I did not want to give it up. I believed that I could keep doing it, but in safer ways. So, I got rid of my unstable concussion board and bought a new highly stable board that I can't ride nearly as fast or as aggressively. I also bought a new helmet, since the old one was pretty banged up. I have been riding this new snowboard for a few years now and have sustained no injuries. It is a new day and I have learned to enjoy snowboarding in a new way. The fork in the road from the concussion helped me to prioritize keeping safe and being less reckless.

As we finish looking at Jacob's conversations with God during the various forks in the road, I also want to point out that he was already in action when he had each of these conversations with God. Jacob wasn't stationary or waiting for God's input or direction at Bethel, Peniel, Mahanaim, or Beersheba. All of these conversations with God happened when Jacob was in motion and going somewhere. I often hear people say that they are waiting for God's input or direction before they make a decision. But with Jacob, we see that he was already on the move when he had his conversations with God. It is easier to steer something that is moving rather than steer something that is stationary.

This same lesson holds true for snowboarding. The slower I move, the more work it takes for me to steer and navigate. In contrast, when I am snowboarding fast, it is significantly less work to maneuver. Let's consider the possibility that God wants us to get moving so that He can begin steering the direction in our lives. Instead of waiting on God for direction, maybe God is waiting on us to move so that we are easier to steer.

This steering lesson is very important for us, as we see demonstrated in Jacob's life. As we survey the entirety of Jacob's life, we see God's conversations with Jacob directing his life at very critical milestones—his young adult years, during his middle age, and at the end of his life. These milestones can also be very similar for us, and we would be wise to have some very strategic and purposeful conversations with God during these milestones.

If you are a young adult, I encourage you to have some in-depth conversations with God about who God has made you to be and about God's ongoing presence with you throughout your life. If you are in the middle-age season of your life, please let God wrestle with you so that your identity doesn't get stuck in the past and sabotage your divine destiny. And if you are in the twilight years of your life as you read this, don't neglect to discuss with God what He has for you in this season so that you fulfill and maximize your impact on the upcoming generation. Our conversations with God at various forks in the road are massively significant!

QUESTIONS FOR REFLECTION

1. In what ways do you need to keep moving or get moving so that God can direct your momentum?

2. How can you be purposeful to dialogue with God at various defining moments in your life?

3. Reflecting on your life, what are some turning points where you have included God? What are some turning points where you didn't include Him?

4. Does darkness make you afraid or uncertain? How can you be certain to have conversations with God during dark or uncertain times in your life?

CONVERSATION STARTER:
ACTION-BASED DIALOGUE

In this chapter, we looked at Jacob wrestling with God and the conversation that grew out of that wrestling experience. This whole wrestling encounter gave me pause as I reflected on the physicality of Jacob's experience. Thinking about Jacob wrestling with God made me think about various physical activities that I have done and the conversations with God that I had during those activities.

A few years ago, I let my physical activity decline because I was busy and had lost interest in exercising. I had a wonderful friend who took me to lunch and encouraged me to take a walk every day. My friend has known me for several decades and I deeply appreciate his care as well as his wisdom. I took his words to heart and began to take daily walks. On these walks, there were some days when I would put in some earbuds and listen to music or a podcast. But the more days I walked, the more I was inclined to walk without audio distraction.

On my walks I began to see, feel, hear, and smell what was around me. I started to smell the sweet blossoms of honeysuckle in the summer and the scent of lavender bushes in the spring. The smell of freshly cut grass reminded me of laying in the grass as a kid, watching the clouds slowly shift, and sensing God's presence in serene contentment. In the fall I would appreciate the changing leaves, and in the winter I would bundle up and breathe in the stillness of the cold.

No matter what the season, hearing the birds chirp, sing, banter, and tweet always brings me joy. Being able to hear hooting owls and cooing doves always makes me smile because of their steady communication regardless of the sun, season, or temperature. Maybe my all-time favorite bird sound is the hummingbird as they buzz through the air. I am always allured by that sound, and I have to pause to look around for their hovering or backward motion. To this day, I am still mesmerized by the agility and flight mobility of hummingbirds.

Not only do I get to enjoy the smells and sounds of nature along my walks, but I also see and appreciate God's creation. I now notice not only the intricate details, but also the broad design. I notice rocks with intricate patterns and tree branches with unique angles or unusual twists. I see flowers or weeds that grow of their own accord in seemingly impossible locations, and I marvel at the tree trunks and bark patterns that reflect strength, age, stability, and endurance. Taking a walk is a visual feast for my eyes and ears that causes me to consider again the creative Source for such a feast. There is much to be said for conversing with God through observing nature and reflecting on God's creative genius that is expressed in the contrasting simplicity and complexity in nature's daily existence.

Besides experiencing and observing nature, my daily walks can often include discussions with God about various struggles or things with which I am wresting. Often I use that time to work out troubling issues, gripe and complain, or discuss with God my problems and frustrations.

I cannot even begin to tell you how many of my walks have started out with me heading out the door, deciding which path to take, and then throwing down with God about some difficulty I am experiencing. I give God an earful about that struggle. In these wrestling conversations with God, He and I have talked about everything from my job, my marriage, my kids, relationships, Saving Moses, internal mindsets, child-hood experiences, weight loss, personal disciplines, sleep struggles, travel experiences, injuries, and loads more!

I am very grateful for these conversations, because they are real, raw, vulnerable, and sincere. Somewhere along the walk and talk, I often open up my soul to God as I begin to feel some dialogue, input, or feedback. I cannot say with certainty when the dialogue with God starts, in terms of hear-ing or sensing God's input; however, as I walk, I get some of the energy of angst worked out enough to where I am in a better place to listen for input from God. Once I have off-loaded all of my words and expended my emotional energy, I am in a more settled place to listen, absorb, and pay atten-tion to God's input.

This form of conversation is very interesting to me because it is organic and relational. I can't really provide you a schematic or roadmap for how to do this kind of conversation. In total disclosure, I often find these to be the messiest, least programed, and most intimate, albeit raw, conversations with God.

I have experienced this way of communicating with God during a variety of life events. For example, when the decision was made to put my dad in an Alzheimer's facility, I took a walk that I will never forget. It was raining that night, and the air was chilled and crisp. I didn't follow a path that I had been on before. To this day I'm not exactly sure where I walked. But I walked for a few hours and cried my eyes out. The rain and drizzle seemed like a good accompaniment to my runny nose and the tears streaming down my cheeks.

Even though I recognized that my dad was aging and that the care that he needed exceeded what we could provide in his own home, I was really unraveled with this decision. Despite all of the logic and reasonable explanations that went into this decision, it was a really hard thing to process and accept. And taking this very long walk gave me the space to wrestle with God, receive divine comfort, be attentive to His presence, and settle into this new reality.

When I returned home from this walk, I was more settled with the decision to make the hard choices that would address my dad's age and declining mental acuity. I had poured out my heart to God and felt His comfort, presence, and attention on that dark and rainy night. This was not an easy conversation, but it was helpful.

In addition to taking walks, I have also that found these kinds of physical activity conversations happen with other exercise methods. For example, from time to time I also enjoy swimming. While it might be a little tricky to get started and the first few laps might be a challenge, I have had some very wonderful and rewarding conversations with God once I found my groove. Those beginning warm-up laps can be time for me to get acclimated to the exercise, the pool temperature, the muscle memory for the various swim strokes, and my workout plan. I have found it to be really helpful to have the rhythm of breathing and swimming strokes as a backdrop for conversations with God. It has been interesting to sense God's presence all around me when I am entirely immersed in the water. I see this as a parallel experience to being immersed in God.

Additionally, when I swim, I have found it to be really helpful to choose a family member to pray for with each lap that I swim. For example, part of my swimming exercise is to do three laps of freestyle swimming with an additional lap with a kick board. For each lap, I bring one of my kids and their needs or concerns before God in prayer. For fifty meters I talk with God about that child. There have been many times when I have sensed God directing me in my conversation or decisions related to that child. Furthermore, I swim additional laps to discuss and pray for my husband, friends, family members, and coworkers.

Not only do I have these activity-based conversations with God when I walk or when I swim, but I have also experienced these kinds of conversations with God when I am snowboarding, shoveling snow, jogging, bike riding, weightlifting, or shooting basketball hoops. I don't understand the science or psychology behind physical activity and conversing with God, but I know that it works.

I suspect you could also have these conversations with God in various activities in your life as well. Maybe such activities could include bike riding, yoga, treadmill exercise, skiing, stretching, hiking, and lots more! I am really excited to present this Conversation Starter to you in hopes that you will explore your own activities and link them to some vibrant, engaging, and transformational conversations with God.

As we finish this chapter, let's remember that Jacob's wrestling conversation with God was one of the most defining moments of his life. In the context of tremendous physical exertion, Jacob's core of his identity was changed, and his walk with God took on new depths and applications that he had not before known or experienced. There is much to be said for conversing with God when we are being physically active!

For further reflection and note-taking see "Action-Based Dialogue" on page 230 in the Epilogue.

5

CAN WE TALK—
MY FUTURE SEEMS BLEAK

When I was a teenager, I had a summer job doing data entry all day. I was massively bored at this job. Each minute seemed to move slower than a sloth, and each hour seemed to stretch well beyond the allotted sixty minutes. Occasionally I would remind myself to be grateful that I had a job and that I was earning money so that I could buy my own car. Despite these reminders, every day that I worked I felt like I was increasingly becoming a zombie who was devoid of energy and enthusiasm. Some days I even felt hopeless.

Usually I could shake myself out of the hopeless feeling by remembering that this was just a summer job and not a life sentence. I would tell myself that school was coming soon, which meant that I could hang out with my friends again and start back into pre-season basketball training.

These reminders would usually shake off the sense of zombie hopelessness that I felt from the daily drudgery of data entry.

If this was how I felt when I was fifteen and struggling with a boring summer job, I can only imagine how Moses felt at eighty years old herding sheep in the wilderness. Despite being afforded the best education and highest leadership training available in his youth, Moses found himself in a dead-end job with no hope of a different future (see Exodus 3–4). I would also suggest that his life had several major contradictions that he wasn't able to reconcile or resolve until well after his first extensive conversation with God.

For example, Moses was born an Israelite who had survived during the period in which Pharaoh had commanded that all baby boys Moses' age be killed. To save his life, his mom had placed him in a basket and put him to float on the Nile river (see Exodus 1:22). Moses was raised and educated in Pharaoh's house, as he had been rescued from the Nile by Pharaoh's daughter even though he was Jewish (see Exodus 2:5-10). In contrast to Moses' comfortable upbringing, his fellow Israelites were in slavery to Pharaoh and were kept in severe bondage.

And probably the exclamation point to punctuate Moses' contradictory existence was when, at forty years old, Moses killed an Egyptian slave master and tried to establish himself as a leader among the Israelites (see Exodus 2:11-14). This whole "uprising" backfired. From this disastrous debacle, Moses fled into the wilderness and spent the next forty years of his life herding sheep, which was obviously a far cry from his cushy and educated upbringing in Pharaoh's palace.

By the time Moses reached eighty years old, I don't think he had much hope for a different future. It is precisely at this point that God interrupts Moses' daily drudgery of walking sheep around, making sure they have food and water, and looking after injured hooves. God confronted Moses with a burning bush that was not consumed by fire (see Exodus 3). Once God knew that He had Moses' attention, He began a conversation with Moses that turned his life upside down. He ended up liberating the Israelites from slavery and establishing Israel as a nation.

At a point of hopelessness in his life, Moses had a conversation with God that turned his life around. In this conversation, Moses joined God for a massively supernatural adventure! The outcomes of Moses' adventure with God could well have surpassed what he had in mind when he killed the Egyptian slave master and tried to establish himself as a leader for Israel at forty years old.

What did God and Moses talk about at this burning bush experience? And how did God break through Moses' hopeless outlook? For starters, the conversation Moses had with God at the burning bush was initiated by God to a very surprised Moses. I think it is really important to consider how this conversation started between God and Moses, because it is possible that we could learn something helpful. *"When the Lord saw that he turned aside to look, God called to him from the midst of the bush and said, 'Moses, Moses!' And he said, 'Here I am'"* (Exodus 3:4). It is significant to recognize that God didn't start talking to Moses until He had Moses' attention. I can look back on my life and see some very important experiences where God talked with me, but only after He had my attention.

A few years ago, for example, I was helping lead a mission trip to Ethiopia. We were staying in an orphanage in the northern part of this magnificent country. During our time there, my friend learned that the orphanage had recently received newborn twin girls. These newborn twins had been abandoned in a field only a few days earlier, and the orphanage where we were staying agreed to accept them. If the orphanage had not received these newborn twins, the police would have been forced to put them back in the field. There were no other options. Needless to say, I was appalled that the survival of these precious babies was at such a high risk, and almost equally aghast that the orphanage had to circumvent their policies to care for these newborns.

What's the point of an orphanage if they don't accept babies? This thought was running through my mind, along with massive maternal feelings. When I popped in to visit these newborns, Sarah and Ruth, I was unraveled. As I held them in my arms, compassion, motherly instincts, nurture, concern, and impulsive care oozed from me. Tears streamed down my face. When I gently returned them to their cribs, I quietly walked out the door.

I had to dial back the intensity of my feelings as I asked the director of the orphanage about his policy for not accepting babies. He graciously explained that the orphanage had very limited resources and had made the decision in the founding days that they would use their limited resources to help the greatest number of children. To do this, they couldn't accept babies, since babies need at least three to five times the resources of an average seven or ten-year-old.

The "coincidence" of meeting Sarah and Ruth was the launch pad that developed my passion for Saving Moses. Saving Moses is the global humanitarian organization I founded to look after the most urgent needs of babies and toddlers in regions around the world where care is least available. If you would like to know more about the journey for Saving Moses, feel free to grab my book *Hanging by a Thread*. Had I not turned aside to visit and meet Sarah and Ruth, I would have missed God speaking to me about His passion and love for babies and toddlers.

In a similar way, God waited to speak to Moses until He knew that Moses was paying attention. Paying attention to God and what He could be saying has to be a critical priority for any conversation we have with Him. Whenever I sense that someone is not listening or paying attention to me, I lose interest in talking with them. Thankfully, God is more patient with us, given how easily distracted we are. Nevertheless, we would be wise to pay attention to our focus and stay attentive in our conversations with God!

Once God saw that Moses was paying attention, He then began to talk. What He said to Moses was nothing less than entirely revolutionary to Moses' perspective at that time. God lets Moses know that He is aware of the suffering and oppression that the Israelites are experiencing at the hands of the Egyptians. And God tells Moses that He is going to liberate the Israelites from Egyptian bondage and bring His people into their own land. God concludes by sharing that

Moses will lead the Israelites out of slavery and into freedom (see Exodus 3:7-9).

Moses counters God's information by asking some important questions about his identity. He asks, *"Who am I?"* (Exodus 3:11). Maybe Moses had a flashback to his disastrous debacle forty years earlier when he killed the Egyptian slave master and was rejected by his own people. Maybe Moses was so bogged down in his own hopeless swamp that he couldn't see a different future. Maybe Moses couldn't see beyond his failures, pain, disappointments, or possible disillusionment to hear God's plan with an open and faith-filled heart. Maybe Moses thought to himself, *I tried to liberate my people a few decades earlier, and it was a fiasco that landed me with these sheep for endless days. I'm not going to make that mistake again.*

Thankfully, God wasn't put off by Moses' questions or his hesitations, excuses, or resistance. If you would be inclined, I encourage you to read the dialogue between Moses and God from Exodus 3:4–4:17. In these verses, Moses and God go back and forth no less than twelve times. Up to this point in the Bible, there had not been such an extensive conversation in one continuous dialogue with God. Over the course of this conversation, Moses is altogether honest with God and puts his reluctance, reasons, and excuses on the table for divine engagement and intervention. Moses lets God know that he is unskilled in speech, that he thinks the Israelite leaders will not listen to him, and that he believes that Pharaoh will not give him the time of day.

God answers each of Moses' arguments and obstacles. He provides supernatural signs for Moses to repeat when necessary, and He provides Moses' brother, Aaron, as a spokesperson. After all of this dialogue, that includes God equipping and persuading him, Moses agrees to do as God has instructed him (see Exodus 4).

We would be wise to take the same lesson to heart. We need to be honest with God about who we are, and we need to communicate our concerns to God. Just like Moses thought that neither the Israelites or Pharaoh would listen to him, we also have people and circumstances around us that could be hostile, skeptical, or dismissive to what we sense God is speaking to us. It is wisdom to communicate these concerns with Him, and it fosters intimacy with Him when we do so.

It is also important to see what happens to Moses over the next several chapters. From his initial conversation with God, Moses connects with Aaron, his brother. In turn, they express God's plan to the Israelite leaders, telling them that He plans to liberate them from the bondage of their Egyptian slavery. Initially, these leaders are receptive to Moses' and Aaron's words, but when Pharaoh hears from Moses and Aaron that they intend to liberate his slaves, he increases the Israelites' workload and hardships (see Exodus 5). When that happens, the leaders of the Israelites get cold feet about going along with Moses' plan. An important lesson to look at is that just because we have a significant and powerful conversation with God does not mean that we will not face opposition or hardships afterward.

For example, I had a really powerful conversation with God the week before I got married. I sensed Him inviting me to join Him in ministry. Subsequent to that conversation,

I had gone through several months of discouraging experiences in relation to God's ministry conversation with me. There were several days when I talked with God, questioned His initial conversation with me, and poured out my heart to Him with honest and raw emotions.

Some of these experiences included getting turned down from doing some Bible teaching, getting the cold shoulder from people with whom I wanted to share Jesus, and being discouraged in my volunteer work in our church's food pantry. I didn't see God opening any doors for me in ministry, and that was difficult for me to reconcile with what I sensed God had been saying to me. The raw emotions I expressed to God included frustration, anger, uncertainty, disappointment, and even some hopelessness from the daily reality of what felt like a mundane existence. When I think back on these seasons in my life, maybe it was a little bit like Moses' shepherding years.

In the next several chapters, God's communication with Moses only relates to the Ten Plagues (see Exodus 8–12). The basic framework is that God speaks and Moses does—command and obedience. Let's appreciate that Moses was able to walk in this unwavering obedience to God without raising questions, resistance, excuses, or doubts most likely because of the intense and deep conversations and interactions that he had previously experienced with God. I suspect that it was also helpful that he saw God confirming his steps of obedience in supernatural ways.

We begin to see more dialogue between Moses and God after He liberated the Israelites from Egyptian slavery with the final plague. The next major hurdle for Moses and the

Israelites was their escape through the Red Sea (see Exodus 14). While standing on the shore of the Red Sea and seeing Pharaoh and his army marching toward them, the Israelites got jittery. When Moses cried out to God, He assured Moses by telling him how He was going to rescue them. Moses again obeys God. In response, God splits the Red Sea, allows the Israelites to pass through freely, and then drowns Pharaoh's army. It was an epic display of God's protection for Israel. As the Israelites continued on their journey, God provided daily manna, quail for meat, and a pillar of cloud by day and fire by night for protection and direction.

The last place where we see Moses have an in-depth conversation with God is after the Israelites messed up with God while Moses was gone for the forty days and nights (see Exodus 33). In this chapter, we see a level of intimacy between Moses and God that is quite extraordinary. Moses pitched a tent outside of the massive Israelite camp as a place for him to get away from the camp activities and have some one-on-one time with God.

> *Whenever Moses entered the tent, the pillar of cloud would descend and stand at the entrance of the tent; and the Lord would speak with Moses. When all the people saw the pillar of cloud standing at the entrance of the tent, all the people would arise and worship, each at the entrance of his tent. Thus the Lord used to speak to Moses face to face, just as a man speaks to his friend...* (Exodus 33:9-11).

I suggest that Moses' conversations with God had been an essential ingredient to his ever-deepening intimacy and connection with God. May the same hold true for us as well as we grow deeper in our walk with God. May His presence become a higher and higher priority among the demands and noises of daily living.

The dialogue between God and Moses that we see in Exodus 33:12-23 reflects a level of trust and connectedness. Instead of Moses being on the receiving end of God giving directions and commands (as we saw in Exodus 3 and 4), Moses appeals to God to accompany the Israelites on their wilderness journey. This conversation grows even more intimate as God speaks to Moses, *"I will also do this thing of which you have spoken; for you have found favor in My sight and I have known you by name"* (Exodus 33:17). For God to remind Moses that He has known him by name is a truly remarkable and intimate statement.

Moses presses for more by asking to see God's glory. God replies that no one can see His face and live, but that He will let Moses see His back as He walks past Moses. These verses have always riveted my attention in terms of having a deep and intimate relationship with God. In fact, the following verse has been a personal goal for me in growing my relationship with God: *"Thus the Lord used to speak to Moses face to face, just as a man speaks to his friend"* (Exodus 33:11).

As we finish this chapter, let me remind you about the first conversation Moses had with God. This was at the burning bush in Exodus 3–4. God started this conversation with Moses when Moses probably felt like his future was hopeless.

And over the course of several conversations with God, along with some very powerful experiences in life, Moses' perspective changed. His tone with God changed from being hopeless to being responsive and engaged with God. And maybe more importantly, Moses was personally changed from these conversations with God. Intimacy with God became a critically essential element to Moses being able to live out God's divine design and call on his life.

QUESTIONS FOR REFLECTION

1. What areas in your life might you consider to be hopeless?

2. What could be some ways that you could eliminate distractions or interruptions that might take away from hearing God speak with you?

3. What areas in your life need some honest conversations with God?

4. Would you want to have a more intimate relationship with God? How could you communicate and demonstrate that desire to God?

CONVERSATION STARTER:
NAMES OF GOD

I am really excited to introduce this Conversation Starter to you because I believe that it will be helpful for you to appreciate with whom you are conversing! I have had conversations with various people over the years who I knew well, only to learn and discover new things about them. It is always fun to learn more about their perspectives, values, background, and their upbringing, all of which helped me understand them more.

For example, I have a friend who always surprises me. Just when I think I know everything about her, I learn something new! Several years ago, when I first began to teach the Bible, I became aware that my speaking abilities were inadequate. A well-intentioned person told me that I slurred by words and didn't annunciate well. Shortly after that, I learned that my friend had been coached in public speaking. She graciously offered to help me with annunciation and articulation. She was massively helpful and a divine provision at that time.

While I knew that side of her very well, I learned a little while later that she had also been to college for business, was abundantly proficient with business operations and execution, and had run her own business. Furthermore, I found out that she was a rodeo champion and had been a doula (birthing coach) for many years. To this day, I keep finding out new and wonderful things about my friend. It is a phenomenal and fun journey! The more I am around her, the more I discover about her. I love the adventure!

If this is true with our human relationships, how much more so can it be in our walk with God? With this Conversation Starter, I use the names of God that are introduced throughout the Old Testament as a platform for you to converse and grow in your connection with Him.

I am presenting this particular Conversation Starter in this chapter because this is how God introduced Himself to Moses. When Moses asked God who he should tell the Israelites sent him, the Bible tells us, *"God said to Moses, 'I AM WHO I AM'"* (Exodus 3:14). The name of God used here is *Jehovah,* and it was first used in the creation story. *"This is the account of the heavens and the earth when they were created, in the day that the Lord God made earth and heaven"* (Genesis 2:4). Jehovah is significant for a few reasons. In Genesis, Jehovah is used in a relational context with Adam and Eve (see Genesis 2:7). Jehovah is also God's covenant name in Genesis 15:4, and it is how God introduces Himself to Moses at the burning bush in Exodus 3:4.

In terms of conversing with Jehovah, I encourage you to sit with the reality that He, the I AM WHO I AM God, is not defined by function, event, object, activity, or relationship. In this part of your conversation with God, you might find it helpful to take some time to sit with this truth: the true God is defined by nothing more than *existence*, and from existence comes a wonderful variety of expressions of *identity*. We will look at many of these expressions in this Conversation Starter, and you will see some great springboards based on God's many names for growing in your conversations with God. The name *Jehovah* can be a launching pad for engaging in conversation with God, as God often attaches another identity of Himself to that root name.

One of those names through which His character can be experienced is *Jehovah Jireh*. Jehovah Jireh means the Lord will provide: *"Abraham called the name of that place The Lord Will Provide, as it is said to this day, 'In the mount of the Lord it will be provided'"* (Genesis 22:14). This is a phenomenal place to start a conversation about God's divine provision in your life. This conversation should not only be in terms of money, but should also be about His provision of time, wisdom, strength, self-control, and more.

When you converse with God about providing resources, I would encourage you not to merely make a "shopping list" of your needs. You will find a conversation with God significantly more fulfilling if you ask Him to show you where He has already been providing for you, so that you can recognize God as your Provider in more real-time living.

The next name of God, *Jehovah Rapha,* can be found in Exodus 15:26: *"…I will put none of the diseases on you which I have put on the Egyptians; for I, the Lord, am your healer."* Jehovah Rapha means the Lord who heals. In this part of your conversation with God, you might find it helpful to look at places in your life where you need healing. This can obviously be physical healing, but it can also include the healing of emotions, memories, spiritual brokenness, relationships, intellectual issues, and more.

After conversing with God about healing, you could continue your pursuit of knowing God through His names by looking at *Jehovah Nissi*. Jehovah Nissi means that God is your banner. *"Moses built an altar and named it The Lord is My Banner"* (Exodus 17:15). Moses experienced God as his banner when the Israelites defeated the Amalekites shortly after leaving their slavery existence in Egypt.

What areas in your life need victory? When we answer this question, our first reaction often is to think of an external situation over which we need victory, such as a relationship or at work. But I strongly encourage you to ask Jehovah Nissi what internal areas in your heart and soul need His victory. These areas can include forgiveness, humility, insecurity, fear, or deception.

Another familiar name of God, *Jehovah Raah*, is found in Psalm 23:1: *"The Lord is my shepherd, I shall not want."* In this part of your conversation with God, you might consider asking God to shepherd your soul. Listen for how God wants to be your Shepherd for this day and for this season in your life. You might consider scanning through Psalm 23 to look at the various functions of a shepherd, and then invite God to shepherd your life in these various ways. A helpful resource to utilize in this part of your conversation is the book *A Shepherd Looks at Psalm 23* by Phillip Keller.

Jehovah Shalom, the Lord is peace, is first introduced in the book of Judges: *"Then Gideon built an altar there to the Lord and named it The Lord is Peace..."* (Judges 6:24). This part of your conversation with God could be a great place to inventory your life to discover places that are not peaceful. Invite Jehovah Shalom to join those places. As you converse with God about what you discover, take some time to listen to and be present with the Lord, your Peace. Sometimes our greatest need for peace is in our own heart and soul.

Possibly one of my favorite names of God is *Jehovah Shammah*, which means the Lord is present. We first read about this name in Ezekiel 48:35: *"...and the name of the city from that day shall be, 'The Lord is there.'"* This name is particularly helpful to refer to when you feel abandoned or neglected. When I have conversations with God about His abiding presence, I have found it helpful to ask Him to show me His presence and participation in those times when I have felt abandonment or neglect. For example, there have been multiple times when I have been traveling by myself to a remote corner of the world for my work with Saving Moses that I have leaned into God. Doing this has chased away feelings of being alone or disconnected from love and relationships.

I couldn't begin to count the number of times I have heard God say to me, "I'm here with you, Sarah" as I was waiting in an immigration line, feeling nervous about a plane connection, riding in a car with a total stranger, or walking down a street overflowing with sewage, garbage, shady people, and erratic drivers. These ongoing conversations with God have really great potential for amazing intimacy and connection with God.

The final Jehovah name we will look at for you to use to spark deep conversations with God is *Jehovah Tsidkenu*, which means the Lord our righteousness. *"...and this is His name by which He will be called, 'The Lord our righteousness'"* (Jeremiah 23:6). Righteous means to live in right standing with God. Ask Him to show you His right standing in your life, along with possible areas and mindsets where you might be trusting in your good works instead of God's righteousness. Without God's righteousness, we are never "good enough." This name can facilitate conversations with God as you explore together what this means and looks like in your life.

In addition to the Jehovah names we just discovered, it is also extremely noteworthy that God's names in the Old Testament include identities associated with the name *Elohim*. This is the first name of God that we read about in the entire Bible: *"In the beginning God created the heavens and the earth"* (Genesis 1:1). Elohim is the name that speaks of the Creator God who made the earth and everything in it. When you converse with God as your Creator, you might consider asking if and what God would want to create in and through you. Sometimes God wants to create solutions through us for the problems, challenges, and needs around us.

After we are introduced to Elohim in Genesis 1:1, the next name of God we read about is *El Elyon*. This name means God Most High. Melchizedek says to Abram, *"And blessed be God Most High, who has delivered your enemies into your hand"* (Genesis 14:20). In this part of your conversation with God, you might find it helpful to take some moments to exalt God for who He is—the Most High. Sit with the sovereignty of God, appreciating that not one thing—no one, no circumstance, no situation, no attitude—nothing is exalted over El Elyon, because God is Most High.

Another name of God for your conversation with Him is *El Roi*. This name means God who sees, and it comes from Genesis 16:13: *"Then she called the name of the Lord who spoke to her, 'You are a God who sees....'"* This name is extremely powerful when we consider the background for its usage. Earlier in Genesis 16, Sarah had offered Hagar, her maidservant, to Abram to produce a son because Sarah wasn't able to get pregnant. Abram agreed to Sarah's suggestion, and Hagar became pregnant. This created intense jealousy in Sarah, so much so that she kicked Hagar out of the house and made her flee into in the wilderness while Hagar was yet pregnant. Hagar was alone in the wilderness, with no resources, no protection, and no place to go. Understandably, she was in great distress when the angel of God appeared to her. Through his words, she came to understand that God sees her.

In a similar way, it is important to talk with God about the fact that He sees you. God is aware of you, knows where you are, is attentive to the circumstances of your life, and is engaged. For this part of your conversation with God, maybe it would be helpful to ask God to make you aware of His attention on and affection for you.

Our final name of God to use as a Conversation Starter is first found in Genesis 17:1: *"Now when Abram was ninety-nine years old, the Lord appeared to Abram and said to him, 'I am God Almighty....'"* *El Shaddai* is the name for God in this passage, and in general terms, it means the all-sufficient one. We can apply this to mean that wherever God is in our lives, there is no deficiency or insufficiency. And of course, this is very comforting.

If we look at this name from a linguistic perspective, El Shaddai in Hebrew means God is the many-breasted one.[1] Clearly, this idea can be unsettling or perplexing, particularly when we consider that much of our thinking about God has more masculine than feminine constructs. Maybe it would be helpful to ask God questions regarding this name. Some questions that could be helpful include:

- "El Shaddai, why am I uncomfortable or unsettled with this name?"
- "El Shaddai, in what ways do I limit Your sufficiency in my life?"
- "El Shaddai, would You please show me the ways in which You have been sufficient in my life?"

We have looked at twelve very unique and powerful names of God. This Conversation Starter has helped us see and explore different expressions and aspects of God's identity. To continue this conversation with God based on His names, consider the following ideas:

- On your phone or in a notebook, list these names and their meanings. Carry them with you to remind you to notice God's presence and how it is integrated into each day.
- Identify the names that are more difficult for you to accept or understand and talk with God about these challenges. Explore the possible reasons for the difficulties and what His solutions might be. How could these names be experienced in your life?
- Identify the names of God that are easy for you to embrace and take some moments to celebrate and

worship God for these characteristics and identities. How do you see them expressed in your life?

- As you listen to friends or family express struggles or needs, consider introducing them to the aspect of God that is expressed in one of His names that could help with that struggle or need.

- Consider taking a different name for every day in a week and pausing to hear or feel what God may be saying to you with each name.

- Remember, the goal of these Conversation Starters is to help you start or continue a conversation with God via unique ways and methods!

For further reflection and note-taking see "Names of God" on page 232 in the Epilogue.

ENDNOTE

1. Kay Arthur, *Lord, I Want to Know You* (Colorado Springs, CO: Waterbrook, 2000), 36-40.

6

CAN WE TALK—
MY LIFE IS IN MELTDOWN

"You lost your job, you learned that your son is addicted to heroin, your wife asked for a divorce after you discovered that she stole your retirement savings, and what you thought were stress-related health struggles were recently diagnosed as a brain tumor." I repeated back my friend's words to him. "Did I get everything right?" I was appalled at hearing him describe how his life was in total meltdown.

"Yep," he replied. "Except you missed that my dog died yesterday."

As I sat with my friend at lunch, I was flabbergasted and speechless. I began to let the gravity of each struggle that he listed sink into my soul, and I started to feel the tremendous burden my friend was shouldering. When I looked into his eyes, I could see the tears on the cusp of overflowing. I could see him steeling himself so that he wouldn't cry in public. His hand was trembling ever so slightly, and he quickly looked away in an attempt to find a distraction so that he could collect his emotions and stay calm, at least on the outside. But I could feel the weight of his soul. It was unnerving to me.

In a similar way, there is a man in the Bible who endured a living hell for a season of his life. We can employ some very helpful applications from observing him. This man's name was Job. And like my friend, he experienced multiple traumas in a short period of time.

Job's life became a virtual hell because of satan's attacks (see Job 1–2). When we find ourselves in these situations, we often ask, "Why?" and try to figure out the cause of such total life meltdown. Thankfully, we get to read about the events and conversations that led up to Job's meltdown—specifically two conversations between God and satan. I don't normally think about these powerful entities talking with each other. Indeed, when I think of Job and the conversations with God that happen in this book, I have always looked at the end of the book.

Upon closer observation, however, it is extremely helpful to consider the initial conversations that happen between God and satan in these beginning chapters. God and satan have two conversations within these chapters, and both happen at God's initiation. The first starts with the question to satan, *"Where have you come from?"* (Job 1:7 New International Version). Satan lets God know that he has been roaming the earth. God then dives into His applause for Job: *"The Lord said to Satan, 'Have you considered My servant Job? For there is no one like him on the earth, a blameless and upright man, fearing God and turning away from evil'"* (Job 1:8).

When I read what God says about Job, it makes me think about God's perspective about him. In God's words to satan about Job, I see no doubt, shame, accusation, condemnation, or hesitation. God does not qualify anything about Job. He does not add a disclaimer like, "For a human, he is a pretty good guy!" If we take God's words at face value, He is massively impressed with Job, even going so far as possibly bragging about Job.

To this end, have you ever thought that God sees you from a very favorable perspective? This might be challenging for you to accept and embrace; however, since First John 4:7 tells us that God is love, then we must consider that genuine love believes the best. "[Love] *bears all things, believes all things, hopes all things, endures all things"* (1 Corinthians 13:7). There is no doubt in my mind that God knew Job even better than Job knew himself. Consequently, God knew all of Job's shortfalls, foibles, quirks, inadequacies, gaps, mistakes, and humanity. In spite of knowing everything about Job, God's words about him to satan were nothing less than total affirmation and applause.

You might want to sit for a few moments to consider the possibility that God knows you better than you know yourself. He thinks highly of you, and He sees you as priceless and infinitely valuable. It is my sincere opinion that if we take this truth to heart, we will have more love in our hearts toward ourselves and others.

Coming back to our story in the book of Job, God asks Satan a question, *"Have you considered My servant Job?"* (Job 1:8). It is after this question that God makes His opinion about Job abundantly clear. In contrast, satan answers God's question with a different point of view. Satan replies,

> *Does Job fear God for nothing? Have You not made a hedge about him and his house and all that he has, on every side? You have blessed the work of his hands, and his possessions have increased in the land. But put forth Your hand now and touch all that he has; he will surely curse You to Your face* (Job 1:9-11).

In contrast to God's affirming posture toward Job, satan is accusatory. In essence, satan tells God that Job is only living an upright life because he has received divine protection and validation. Satan tells God that if Job's life goes into meltdown, Job will give up his righteous posture and curse God. Satan's words express his perspective, which is grounded in accusation, condemnation, judgment, hostile separation, and destruction. Even worse, Satan throws down a challenge about Job. He wagers that if bad circumstances were to surround Job, he would turn away from God.

In the following verses, God gives satan permission to remove Job's privileged existence in an attempt to reveal what was really in Job's heart.

Thus, begins the meltdown. In one day, Job loses all of his massive wealth and all of his children. Despite such severe tragedies, Job continues to keep his faith in God. He does not turn away from serving God, nor does he let his relationship with God become merely transactional. The hardships reveal that Job's commitment to God is not based on what he gets from Him or on whether or not he can live comfortably without pain, suffering, deprivation, or crisis.

After Job endures the series of tragedies, he is once again the topic of conversation between God and satan (see Job 2). This conversation plays out in similar ways to the first conversation between God and satan. Indeed, God's words to satan are verbatim from chapter 1, with the additional observation that despite satan's efforts of creating heartache and meltdown in Job's life, he still maintains his integrity. And similar to how satan replied to God in chapter 1, satan continues to accuse, belittle, and look for opportunities to hurt Job. Satan says to God, *"Skin for skin! Yes, all that a man has he will give for his life. However, put forth Your hand now, and touch his bone and his flesh; he will curse You to Your face"* (Job 2:4-5).

God tells satan that he may attack Job's body, but he may not take Job's life. Consequently, satan gives Job very painful boils over all his body. We need to take a moment to imagine a man who has lost all of his wealth, all of his kids, and now he is covered in open sores. Because of all of this misery, grief, and tragedy, Job's wife's advice was that he should curse God and die. Even so, Job did not curse God.

In this state of total meltdown, Job's friends show up in his life, presumably to be present and helpful. They spend a week with him in silence as they observe Job's incredible suffering. After this period, they start talking with him. In fact, the next thirty-five chapters are conversations that happen among Job and his friends. From my opinion, these friends model everything we should *not do* when someone's life is in meltdown mode. Job's friends accuse him of wrongdoing based on their belief that tragedy happens in people's lives as a direct result of bad behavior.

In reply, Job defends himself. This difference in beliefs about tragedy is discussed in a back-and-forth dialogue between Job and his friends for the majority of this book. Ultimately, they come to terms with some irreconcilable differences of opinions and perspectives. Thankfully, God steps into the mix as the final authority. Things begin to change when God and Job begin talking.

In my own life, I have seen that conversations with God are essential if I am going to come through meltdown seasons without being destroyed by hardship and adversity. Over the course of about one year, for example, right about the time when my daughter was starting high school, all kinds of terrible things happened. I sustained a severe concussion from a snowboarding accident, my husband had a minor stroke, one of my kids had a grand mal seizure, our finances were squeaky tight, and our neighbors, who were best friends to our family, moved to a different state. All of these experiences were in addition to the normal work pressures and demands that we carried in day-to-day living. Thankfully, in contrast to Job's prickly and accusatory friends, most of my friends were compassionate, supportive, and patient with me during this meltdown season.

There are many helpful lessons to apply when we or our friends go through horrific experiences or have seasons of meltdown. We should:

- Recognize the season and appreciate that it is temporary—even though it might feel as if it is a permanent situation.

- Be steady and compassionate with a friend who is going through a meltdown season.

- Not allow our perspectives on God to change based on our circumstances or feelings.

- Not expect everyone to understand or be sympathetic with our feelings or experiences.

- Trust that God can use everything to be of benefit to us—even hardships—as long as we stay in love with God and stay true to His designs and purposes in our lives (see Romans 8:28-29).

The chapters in Job that express the conversations that happen between Job and his friends can be helpful to us when we are going through difficult seasons and experiences. What I believe is even more helpful, however, is the conversation that happens between Job and God in the last several chapters of this book.

GOD'S CONVERSATION WITH JOB

When all of Job's friends had spoken their piece with him, God wades into the fray and speaks to Job. The place from which God speaks is a whirlwind (see Job 38:1). It is noteworthy to me that God begins His interaction with Job from the midst of a whirlwind and not from a place of serenity or quiet repose. When we go through a season of meltdown in our lives, it can often seem to be a very tumultuous time, replete with upheaval, uncertainty, chaos, and impending disaster. In the midst of not only the meltdown of Job's life, but also in a very stormy time, *God speaks*.

I pray that this observation resonates in your heart, particularly if your life is presently stormy, is overflowing with chaos, or is coming apart at the seams. God can and does speak during a storm—not just during sunny and serene days. It is possible, however, that we could miss God speaking to us because we are avoiding storms, living hunkered down in a storm-free lifestyle. Let's keep in mind that God can speak to us, even in stormy seasons!

Let's also consider that when God begins to speak with Job, His words do not seem very comforting. Indeed, God commands Job to, *"Pull yourself together, Job! Up on your feet! Stand tall! I have some questions for you, and I want some straight answers"* (Job 38:2-3 The Message). When I think about God's initial words to Job, they don't feel nurturing or soothing. Perhaps God speaks this way to accentuate the contrast that God's message to Job will not be anything like what his friends had to say to him. It is one thing to have dialogue with friends who are equal in our humanity who have similar flaws and failures, but it is another to have a conversation with the Creator of the universe who is the all-knowing God.

When we converse with God, we are not talking with an equal counterpart, and we are not having a horizontal dialogue. May we always stay in this proper vertical alignment in the midst of deeply intimate and vulnerable conversations with God!

Once this alignment has been clarified, God asks Job an extensive series of questions. He begins questioning Job by asking about his presence and participation at the creation of the earth, the sea, morning, stars, weather, and wild animals. God continues to ask Job if he's able to look after various wild animals, knowing their habits and routines. Clearly, the answer to these questions is no. Job is not on the same level as God.

After God finishes with this first long list of questions, Job then tells God that he realizes that he is insignificant compared to Him. Furthermore, Job assures God that, even though Job has vented and expressed himself, he will not continue to make a case nor defend his position. He is clear that God is sovereign and there is nothing more to add.

God, however, continues to question Job. He asks Job, out of a storm again, about Job's ability to implement justice and deal with proud and humble men. God also questions Job about whether or not he has the power or ability to overtake two fierce, intimidating, and mighty animals— the Leviathan and the Behemoth. Modern scholars don't entirely agree on what these two animals were; but from God's questions, it is abundantly clear that these animals were very ferocious!

God again makes the point to Job that he is a frail human going through a hellacious season, but that ultimately God is sovereign. All total, God asks Job more than seventy questions. Job's final concluding words with God express that he acknowledges God's sovereignty and postures himself in the position of being a student to God's ways.

After this, God instructs Job's friends to make things right with him since they had been combative and unhelpful. In return, God instructs Job to pray for his friends: *"The Lord restored the fortunes of Job when he prayed for his friends, and the Lord increased all that Job had twofold"* (Job 42:10).

When we finish looking at this conversation between God and Job, we would be wise to digest and apply a few essential takeaways. To begin, life has meltdown seasons even when we are doing our best to live in a way that pleases God. Also, no matter what happens, His love for us doesn't change. God's character is more reliable than our circumstances that frequently do change. Finally, no matter what we go through, God is sovereign, all-knowing, and always present with us. To this end, let's trust God more than we trust our feelings or circumstances.

All of God's questions to Job have caused me to pause and reflect. For being all-knowing, God sure asks Job a lot of questions! And the quantity of God's questions that He asked Job led me to think about why God would ask these questions when He already knows the answers. As I thought about God asking questions of Job, I remembered that we already looked at how God initiated the conversation with Adam using a question: Where are you? God also initiated the conversation with Cain with a question, and God continued to question Cain even after he killed his brother. And God asked Abraham, Jacob, and Moses questions as well. There is repetition in God's method of starting communication with us with questions.

Why would God ask us questions when He already knows the answers and knows us? As humans, we often use questions to get information or assistance. Questions are also essential ingredients for relationship development and intimacy. And questions can facilitate conversations that help us connect with others and deepen relationships.

For example, I have a friend who asks questions like she breathes air. She starts with easy stuff like, "How did you sleep? What are you making for dinner? Where are you traveling?"

She has a knack for starting with these kinds of surface questions and then asking deeper questions like, "Why do you think that way? How did that experience or conversation make you feel? Why are you being aloof with me?"

Being on the receiving end of these questions has provoked me to ask like-minded questions and to make deeper inquiries with the hope of making closer connections and increasing intimacy. Questions are a phenomenal way to grow and deepen our relationships.

I see God use this same principle in His conversations with us. Ultimately, when I look at the questions that God asks Adam, Cain, Abraham, Jacob, Moses, and Job, they are relationship questions that seek to connect each man with God more deeply.

Consider God's questions to each man:

- To Adam in Genesis 3:9: *"Where are you?"*
- To Cain in Genesis 4:6: "Why are you angry? And why has your countenance fallen?"

- To Cain after he killed Abel in Genesis 4:9: *"Where is Abel your brother?"*
- To Abraham in Genesis 18:9: *"Where is Sarah your wife?"*
- To Abraham in Genesis 18:13: *"Why did Sarah laugh?"*
- To Abraham in Genesis 18:14: "Is anything too difficult for the Lord?"
- To Jacob in Genesis 32:27: *"What is your name?"*
- To Moses in Exodus 3–4: There is a long conversation between God and Moses where questions are asked and answered.
- To Job in Job 38–41: God asks Job more than seventy questions.

While it is interesting to think about the kind of questions that God asks us and why He asks them, it is also helpful to think about the questions we ask God and why we ask these questions. Let's be careful that we ask God questions for the purpose of getting to know Him better and to deepen our relationship and connection with God.

In my life, there have been seasons when I have asked God questions that were filled with accusation, like how He could be loving but allow atrocities. While I know it is likely all of us have asked God this question or similar questions, nevertheless, let us prioritize our questions toward growing in intimacy with Him rather than demanding God explain or justify Himself.

The following are some ideas for asking God questions:

- Where are You in this circumstance? Where were You when that difficulty happened in my life?
- How are You demonstrating love in this situation?
- What are You saying to me through the conversation with that person?
- What would You have me say or do at this time?
- How can I know You better in this season?
- Would You please help me to recognize You better?

In our conversations with the triune God, let's remain committed to His purposes for growing deeper and deeper in our relationship with Him, regardless of what we go through in life. This is important, regardless of the seasons or circumstances of our lives—and it is not solely dependent on our feelings or moods. God is asking us to join the conversation for a deeper connection and intimacy with Him. Will you say yes?

CONVERSATION STARTER:
MEDITATIVE REFLECTION

"I know what I'm supposed to do, but I'm having a hard time doing it!" Have you thought or said this a few times in your life? This was part of a conversation I had with a friend when I was being really vulnerable about a personal struggle regarding my weakness and inability to change.

"Sarah, have you ever tried meditating on the Bible?" Her question conjured up images of monks in orange robes who were cross-legged, humming "Om" with their eyes closed, and oblivious to their surroundings.

I guess my friend could see by the reaction on my face that I was kind of skeptical about her suggestion. She quickly added, "Not like Eastern meditation found in Hinduism or Buddhism, but more like zeroing in on some Bible verses to give your brain a focal point."

Her description briefly reminded me about the Sunday School memory verse experiences where I mindlessly recited various Bible verses to get the gold star on a chart by my name or to win a reward like candy or a toy. So again, I was skeptical of her suggestion.

Thankfully, she didn't get discouraged by my skepticism. She continued to explain her idea so I could try something that I would discover to be a richly rewarding and deeply satisfying conversational experience with God.

What does a conversation with God look like when we do the meditating thing?

I would like to walk you through an example of a conversation where meditating on a Bible passage is used. I use Psalm 40:1-2 as our example since I have been walking with God through these verses for a few months now.

If you are just starting out using meditation as a way to converse with God, here are a few quick tips that could be helpful:

- Start out with a small increment of time, like ten minutes. When you have built up some continuity with this method of conversation, you might consider

increasing the amount of time that you spend in
increments of five minutes.

- Find a quiet place that has as few distractions as
possible. This could be your car with the engine off,
an unused office or classroom at school, or a quiet
area in your living space.

- Put your phone on airplane mode to minimize
interruptions.

- Have some paper and a pen readily available to write
down what you hear and what is noteworthy. Using a
paper and pen eliminates the temptation to use your
phone for notes, which could make it easier for you to
be distracted by emails or text messages.

- Figure out the time of day in which you are the most
alert and use this time to meditate.

- Be committed to trying this type of conversation
for at least five days. It seems to take that long to
create an honest experience that is not rushed or
transactional.

- Be sure to use a Bible translation that is comfortable
and engaging for you. Do not use a translation that is
stiff, complicated, or difficult to absorb.

- As a way of holding yourself accountable, consider
asking a friend to check in with you to see if you are
practicing this type of conversation.

- Start each ten-minute practice with a prayer asking
God to help you pay attention and be present in the
conversation.

Let's jump into this Conversation Starter using the New International Version of Psalm 40:1-2 as a sample dialogue: *"I waited patiently for the Lord; he turned to me and heard my cry. He lifted me out of the slimy pit, out of the mud and mire; he set my feet on a rock and gave me a firm place to stand."*

When I begin a conversation with God, I take the first phrase and sit with it for some time: *"I waited patiently for the Lord."* That is exactly what I do—I wait patiently for the Lord. When my mind gets distracted with things like the grocery list, demands from work, kid activities, housecleaning, etc., I ask for Holy Spirit to help me wait patiently, and I return to sitting with God.

With the various distractions that come up, I have discovered a few things that help me deal with them. For example, when I remember something I need to do, instead of getting anxious about when and how I am going to get that done, I write that task on a piece of paper so I can consider it later. Also, when I find my attention wandering down some mental rabbit trail, I don't let myself get upset or disappointed. Such emotional responses are not helpful and only make it more difficult to come back to being present with God. Furthermore, I have learned that spending time with God, waiting patiently for the Lord, is not a waste of time. Keeping company with God is constructive, soothing, rejuvenating, illuminating, and grounding.

After some moments of waiting, I will look at the next phrase in Psalm 40:1: *"He turned to me and heard my cry."* I take some time to ponder and settle into that phrase. I think about experiences where I know that God has turned to me and heard my cry. Such experiences include sensing God in my emotions when I am upset with someone, feeling as if God organized my schedule for the day so that I would have some unexpected and helpful breaks, and having wisdom or clarity in a difficult or confusing situation.

What could God turning to you look like in your life? Maybe it would be beneficial to ask God to show you where He has turned to you and heard your cry. Many times, this is a better way to talk with God rather than itemizing all the negativities and deficiencies in your life. It has been my experience that when I look for God's presence in my life, I find Him showing up in many creative and unexpected ways.

As I continue to meditate on Psalm 40, I slowly move into the first phrase of the second verse that says, *"He lifted me out of the slimy pit, out of the mud and mire."* When I settle into this verse, I look at some places in my life that could be slimy pits, mud holes, and quagmires. I ask Holy Spirit to point out these places to me, because sometimes I can deceive myself. Some muddy pits that God has pointed out to me have included gossipy habits, negative thought patterns about various people, bad routines with time management, conversations that have ongoing toxic bends, hurtful eating habits that reflect poor discipline, and insecurities and fears that have dominated decisions.

Upon recognizing these muddy pits, I reach out to God and ask for help to lift me out of these slimy pits. And because I have a vivid imagination, I see myself lifting up my hand and asking for help. I then imagine God's hand grabbing mine and literally pulling me out the mud and slime. I imagine rinsing off what is still clinging to me, washing off a foul odor and muddy appearance.

Having been extracted from the slime pit, the next phrase says, *"He set my feet on a rock and gave me a firm place to stand"* (Psalm 40:2). As I meditate on this phrase, I think about what it would look and feel like to stand on a rock rather than sink into a muddy quagmire. For example, rather than having conversations that include gossip, God can help me steer the topics to more stable or constructive content. Instead of wallowing in hurtful eating habits, I ask for God's strength to resist the temptation to eat junk food. And in this part of the conversation with God, I ask Him to help me imagine what it would look like to walk on solid ground in these difficult areas in my life. I have found it very helpful to imagine what these quagmires could look like as firm ground instead of destructive pits.

Hopefully, this example of meditating on Scripture verses has given you some encouragement for what this conversation with God could look like for you. I am very excited for you to explore this conversation on your personal journey and dialogue with God. I have used this way of conversing with God for many decades and it has been immensely helpful to me!

As I finish with this Conversation Starter, I want to leave you with some suggestions for Bible passages that you could explore for your own conversations with God. The following verses are from various parts of the Bible. I have learned that the Bible is overflowing with incredible jewels and wonderful opportunities to discover and revel in God's presence. Enjoy!

IDEAS FOR MEDITATING VERSES

Exodus 15:2-3: *"The Lord is my strength and song, and He has become my salvation; this my God, and I will praise Him; my father's God, and I will extol Him. The Lord is a warrior; the Lord is His name."*

2 Chronicles 14:11: *"Then Asa called to the Lord his God and said, 'Lord, there is no one besides You to help in the battle between the powerful and those who have no strength; so help us, O Lord our God, for we trust in You, and in Your name we have come against this multitude. O Lord, You are our God; let not man prevail against You.'"*

Job 23:10-12: *"But He knows the way I take; when He has tried me, I shall come forth as gold. My foot has held fast to His path; I have kept His way and not turned aside. I have not departed from the command of His lips; I have treasured the words of His mouth more than my necessary food."*

Psalm 25:4-5: *"Make me know your ways, O Lord; teach me Your paths. Lead me in Your truth and teach me, for You are the God of my salvation; for You I wait all the day."*

Isaiah 50:4-5: *"The Lord God has given Me the tongue of disciples, that I may know how to sustain the weary one with a word. He awakens Me morning by morning, He awakens My ear to listen* *as a disciple. The Lord God has opened My ear; and I was not disobedient nor did I turn back."*

Matthew 5:14-16: *"You are the light of the world. A city set on a hill cannot be hidden; nor does anyone light a lamp and put it under a basket, but on the lampstand, and it gives light to all who are in the house. Let your light shine before men in such a way that they may see your good works, and glorify your Father who is in heaven."*

1 Corinthians 13:4-7: *"Love is patient, love is kind and is not jealous; love does not brag and is not arrogant, does not act unbecomingly; it does not seek its own, is not provoked, does not take into account a wrong suffered, does not rejoice in unrighteousness, but rejoices with the truth; bears all things, believes all things, hopes all things, endures all things."*

Ephesians 3:16-19: *"That He would grant you, according to the riches of His glory, to be strengthened with power through His Spirit in the inner man, so that Christ may dwell in your hearts through faith; and that you, being rooted and grounded in love, may be able to comprehend with all the saints what is the breadth and length and height and depth, and to know the love of Christ which surpasses knowledge, that you may be filled up to all the fullness of God."*

For further reflection and note-taking see "Meditative Reflection" on page 236 in the Epilogue.

7

CAN WE TALK—
MY PLANS ARE CHANGING

"Let's have SIX kids!" I declared to my husband after giving birth to our daughter, Isabell. My pregnancy with her had been smooth, and I found myself thoroughly committed to having lots of kids! This desire, however, was a drastic change of plans from what my husband and I had discussed previously. When we were first married, we had been somewhat cautious and very logical about having and raising kids, and the possibility of having children had been an ongoing discussion for some years. After having been married for more than five years, my husband and I had agreed at the same time to start having kids.

He now was faced with me changing the plans in a sudden and enthusiastic about-face. Thankfully, he didn't freak out because of this massive shift. Maybe he concluded that since I was well into my 30s that time was of the essence and that this was the season in our lives for being pregnant and having babies. Whatever the reason, he was not resistant to my new plans.

In rapid succession, we had three kids each eighteen months apart. By the time I finished delivering my third baby, I was very tired. I decided that three kids—not six kids—was our final number.

Changing plans for some people can be loads of fun and an adventure in the making. On the other hand, changing plans for other folks can be excruciating or even debilitating. So, what does a conversation with God look like when plans change? And perhaps an even more poignant question would be, what does conversation with God look like when God changes our plans? How do we talk with God about our plans that He changes?

There are some helpful verses that we could consider, including:

- Proverbs 16:9: "The mind of man plans his way, but the Lord directs his steps."
- Isaiah 55:8-9: "'For My thoughts are not your thoughts, nor are your ways My ways,' declares the Lord. 'For as the heavens are higher than the earth, so are My ways higher than your ways and My thoughts than your thoughts.'"
- Proverbs 16:1: "The plans of the heart belong to man, but the answer of the tongue is from the Lord."
- Proverbs 19:21: "Many plans are in a man's heart, but the counsel of the Lord will stand."

When we read these verses, we can usually agree that God is sovereign and that our plans are ultimately subject to His authority and direction. However, taking this truth from theory and living it on practical terms can be challenging. To help with these challenges, I suggest that we look at Samuel in the Old Testament. His story can help us blend theoretical acceptance into daily reality and have a glimpse into what conversations with God can look like when God changes our plans.

The first conversation that we read about between God and Samuel happens when Samuel is a little boy (see 1 Samuel 3). To understand the significance of this conversation, it is helpful to have a little bit of background context. Samuel was a little boy who was fervently prayed for by his mother, Hannah: *"O Lord of hosts, if You will indeed look on the affliction of Your maidservant and remember me, and not forget Your maidservant, but will give Your maidservant a son, then I will give him to the Lord all the days of his life, and a razor shall never come on his head"* (1 Samuel 1:11).

After weaning Samuel, Hannah brought him to the tabernacle and dedicated him to the Lord. She left Samuel there to serve and to be trained under the leadership of Eli, the high priest. Samuel slept next to the Ark of the Covenant in the tabernacle (1 Samuel 3:3). I think it's important to get our children around God's presence as much and as soon as possible during their childhood.

I had the luxury of growing up as a pastor's kid. During the weekdays, I had the run of the church. Of course, I tried to play with the toys in the nursery when I wasn't supposed to, but I also was able to hang out in the sanctuary when no one else was there. In these lingering times, I could sense God in that space very clearly and strongly. I will never forget going into the sanctuary as a little girl and feeling God through a sense of awe, deep peace, and pervasive love. Even as I write about this memory now, I can sense the residue of those feelings and memories.

I also remember having friends who would run around the church with me both on Sundays and during the week. Looking back, I realize that many of the parents of my friends wanted their kids to be around God's presence as much as possible. I am totally convinced that our kids can experience God for themselves at young ages. Those experiences can help them start their own lifelong conversations with God.

God's conversation with Samuel started when he was a young boy. One night as Samuel was sleeping, he heard his name (see 1 Samuel 3). He jumped up and ran to Eli replying, "Here I am." Eli tells Samuel that he did not call him and that he should return to bed. This happens two more times, at which point Eli discerns that it is God who is speaking to Samuel, and he coaches Samuel how to reply. The fourth time God calls Samuel, he replies, *"Speak, for Your servant is listening"* (1 Samuel 3:10). Samuel's conversation with God begins, and this is when Samuel hears that God is changing the plans for Eli's successor.

Prior to God's conversation with Samuel, the standard succession plan for a high priest was to pass his position to his oldest son. This was similar to the idea of a king's son becoming the king when his dad died. There was a general expectation that one of Eli's sons would become the next high priest; however, Eli's sons didn't fear God. They used their position for personal benefit. This was extremely displeasing to God, and He shared that with Samuel (see 1 Samuel 3:11-14).

DISCERNMENT

Discernment is a critical ingredient in our conversations with God, particularly when we see that our plans are being changed. In this recorded conversation, God called Samuel's name three consecutive times. Even when Samuel didn't recognize who was calling him, God waited for Samuel to discern His voice before any conversation began. This idea of repetition or echo has been very helpful to me as I am growing to recognize when God is speaking with me. In my daily living, this plays out for me when I see or hear the same thing several times.

For example, I repeatedly felt a nudge regarding one of my friends possibly writing a book. I did not talk with him about it because I was aware that such a nudge could easily be my own idea. I like to write and am an author, therefore, I knew that I could be projecting my own preferences on my friend. But I kept feeling this nudge, and it was growing stronger and happening at unexpected times—repetition. When I had the chance to tell him that I felt that he was sup-posed to write a book, he was totally onboard. "Yeah, Sarah. I know I'm supposed to write a book. God has spoken this to me many times through many different people." Similar to Samuel hearing his name four times, I find confidence in knowing that God is speaking to me when He confirms His words by repetition.

Another principle that helps us discern God's voice is listening. When Eli coached Samuel on how to reply to God, Eli told Samuel to say, *"Speak, Lord, for your servant is listening"* (1 Samuel 3:9). As I have grown in my walk with God, I have come to understand that the more I listen *for* God's voice, the easier it gets to listen *to* God's voice. In order to have a conversation with God, it is important to discern His voice. This is all the more so when our plans are changing!

Upon hearing about God's change of plans, Samuel communicates what he has heard to Eli who takes God's word at face value. After Samuel's conversation with God, Eli's sons go into battle and are killed, the Ark of the Covenant gets captured, and Eli falls backward, breaks his neck, and dies. Clearly these events are tragic, but maybe God's conversation with Samuel before these events helped Samuel's heart to be settled in the midst of such change. As a result, Samuel became the de facto leader of Israel for many years.

Samuel's role of leadership remained until God orchestrated another divine change of plans. In First Samuel 8, we read that Samuel had been Israel's leader for many years. He was planning to pass on his leadership responsibilities to his two sons, Joel and Abijah; however, the elders of Israel informed Samuel that his sons were unacceptable. The elders said that Samuel's sons perverted justice and didn't behave with the same integrity as Samuel. Furthermore, the elders were very clear with Samuel that they wanted a king as his replacement instead of his sons.

The decision of the elders was hard for Samuel to hear. He told the Lord what he was feeling, and God responded by saying,

> *Listen to the voice of the people in regard to all that they say to you, for they have not rejected you, but they have rejected Me from being king over them. Like deeds which they have done since the day that I brought them up from Egypt even to this day—in that they have forsaken Me and served other gods—so they are doing to you also* (1 Samuel 8:7-8).

I really like this conversation between Samuel and God because we get to see Samuel express his pain to God about Israel rejecting his plans. God not only steps into Samuel's hurt by identifying with the rejection that he was feeling, but He also expresses the rejection that He experienced from His people. This conversation encourages me that I can talk with God about my emotions, and He can be right there with me in my feelings. God is not unraveled, dismayed, repelled, or disappointed by our feelings. Our emotions can be an integral part of our conversations with God.

PREFERENCE

After Samuel and God talk about Israel's rejection, God explains the process of selecting the next leader and the practical implications of that process. It is noteworthy that both Samuel and Israel have assumptions that they have already made about who should be the next leader, even before they consider God's input or preference. Indeed, Samuel never asks God about who his successor should be. It seems he assumes that his sons, Joel and Abijah, will be Israel's next leaders.

The leaders of Israel also never ask for God's direction or preference for their next leader. Instead, they look at the leadership structure of the neighboring nations as a benchmark to tell Samuel that they want a king instead of Samuel's sons. The leaders of Israel wanted to conform to what they saw in the surrounding nations.

In God's conversation with Samuel on this topic, He changes Samuel's plan to use his sons, as well as the leaders' plan to have a king. God acknowledges the need for the next leader of Israel, but He makes the decision Himself. In the end, God lets Samuel know that He has chosen a leader. It won't be Samuel's sons: *"About this time tomorrow I will send you a man from the land of Benjamin, and you shall anoint him to be prince over My people Israel..."* (1 Samuel 9:16).

The central takeaway that we can apply to our lives from the dialogue between Samuel and God about leadership succession is this: it is essential to ask God for His preferences in our conversations and not just assume that He will be in agreement with our plans. If we do not ask for God's input, we will find ourselves on thin ice. If we rely on tradition, the way it has always been, or conformity to the social norms as our guiding principles in life, we may miss God's best. Later we read that Saul was chosen and anointed to be king over

Israel, but in these initial conversations, God's input clearly changed Samuel's plans.

SELECTION

In the final conversation between Samuel and God, we read how God gave Samuel direction about how to select a replacement for Saul:

> *Now the Lord said to Samuel, "How long will you grieve over Saul, since I have rejected him from being king over Israel? Fill your horn with oil and go; I will send you to Jesse the Bethlehemite, for I have selected a king for Myself among his sons." But Samuel said, "How can I go? When Saul hears of it, he will kill me." And the Lord said, "Take a heifer with you and say, 'I have come to sacrifice to the Lord.' You shall invite Jesse to the sacrifice, and I will show you what you shall do; and you shall anoint for Me the one whom I designate to you"* (1 Samuel 16:1-3).

I appreciate that the dialogue between Samuel and God includes Samuel's concern about the possible consequences he could experience for being obedient to God. This dialogue shows us that God is not only concerned about the big picture of getting a replacement king for Israel, but it shows us that God is also concerned about the day-to-day practicalities of keeping Samuel out of harm's way with Saul. This reminds me that God is attentive to our daily concerns.

Furthermore, the conversation between God and Samuel gets extremely powerful when Samuel sits down with Jesse and his sons to listen for God's selection for Israel's next king. Samuel asks Jesse to bring out each of his sons to see which one God would choose to be king. When Jesse's oldest son stands before Samuel, he has an insightful conversation with God.

> *When they entered, he looked at Eliab and thought, "Surely the Lord's anointed is before Him." But the Lord said to Samuel, "Do not look at his appearance or at the height of his stature, because I have rejected him; for God sees not as man sees, for man looks at the outward appearance, but the Lord looks at the heart"* (1 Samuel 16:6-7).

I find that the wisdom God gave to Samuel is timeless and universal for many of the decisions that we make. I think this is particularly true when we judge people. We have a tendency to be influenced by the first impressions of what we see or hear.

This reminds me of a friend I met several years ago when I was ministering at a church in the United States. Following the Sunday evening service, the pastor and his wife took me out for dinner and invited their adult son to join us. This son was a nice guy, but he did not seem particularly interested in topics of spiritual significance. It seemed like he was solely into fast cars and motorcycles. This didn't bother me in any way, because he was a kind and interesting person who was enjoying life.

I have stayed in touch with this family, and over the years the son has talked with me numerous times. He brings up what he has been learning about Jesus, what he has been reading in the Bible, and how God is directing his steps, his prayers, and the burdens on his heart. I am abundantly grateful that I didn't dismiss this wonderful man from the outset. It would have been easy to do if I had been looking and listening to only what I could see and hear on the surface. Indeed, this man encourages and inspires me to live in full pursuit of God, no matter what circumstances or experiences I might be going through at any given time.

To this end, we need to guard against the societal norm or conventional wisdom that merely looks at a person's clothing, haircut, initial communication abilities, or visual presentation. If God doesn't make assessments based on a person's appearance or initial presentation, neither should we.

Another important thing to consider in Samuel's dialogue with God is how long this conversation lasted. Once Jesse's sons started passing before Samuel, God's input to Samuel was a consistent no. After God tells Samuel that Eliab is not the correct choice, He continues to say no to each of the next five sons of Jesse. It is possible that Samuel could have been increasingly unsettled by God's continual answer of no to each of Jesse's sons.

I can imagine that as Samuel had Jesse's sons lined up in front of him and God kept telling him no to each son, maybe Samuel began to think that they were running out of options. I think that is an important point to consider in our conversations with God. There have been times when I have talked really passionately with God and explained that, because I couldn't see any more options or opportunities, God had failed and messed up.

This was a lesson I learned when my daughter was entering kindergarten. I had done some legwork, along with much prayer, in the hopes of getting my daughter into a local and popular charter school. As the first day of school approached, her name sat on a waiting list. It looked highly improbable that there would be an open slot for her. I began to scurry around and explore different options for her schooling. As I researched options, it was increasingly clear that she would be able to attend no school other than our local public school. She began her first day of kindergarten there, and even though the school was a good option, I was pretty disappointed with God.

I resigned myself to our daughter attending our local public school, and began looking at various ways I could get involved. I was hopeful that my volunteer service would be helpful to the school. After about one week, I received a call from the charter school. The nice lady explained that a slot had opened in their kindergarten program and she asked if I was still interested in my daughter attending this charter school. I quickly accepted the offer and our daughter switched attendance to this school. This school was a great blessing to our family for many years. Sometimes when we hear an answer of no from God, it is an opportunity for us to grow in our faith. Sometimes we must trust God for a different yes or different timing.

Even after Samuel heard God say no to each of Jesse's seven sons, he persisted and asked Jesse if these were all of his kids. Jesse replied that he had one more son, the youngest who was herding sheep. Samuel requested that this youngest son be brought in to see if he might be God's selection. When the youngest son, David, came in, God made it clear to Samuel that He had selected David to be king. Samuel anointed David in the midst of his older brothers (see 1 Samuel 16:12-13).

I am grateful for the conversation between Samuel and God about who God had selected to be the next king of Israel. It helps me appreciate that we can dialogue with God about decisions that we need to make when we face forks in the road on our journey of life. The interaction that we can have with God at these junctures can help us learn more about God and bring us to better results than if we persist in doing life under the limits of our human wisdom and strength. Indeed, God's ways are higher than our ways!

QUESTIONS FOR REFLECTION

1. When you make plans and they change, what could a conversation with God look like?

2. In what specific areas of your life would it be helpful to have more discernment to recognize God's voice and input?

3. If you can choose among societal norms, family tradition, or God's input and/or preference, which of these three would be your instinctual choice? In what ways could you begin pursuing God's preferences more consistently?

4. When is it easiest for you to be persuaded by someone's image or exterior presentation? Good looks? Nice clothing? Convincing intelligence? What are some ways you could prioritize God's input over the appealing image a person might present?

CONVERSATION STARTER:
LORD'S PRAYER

Jesus had many conversations with His disciples when He lived among us. He told them lots of stories or parables, He corrected their faulty thinking, and He invited them to join Him in a lifetime of miracles and adventures. He also answered lots of questions about sin, divine provision, and miracles, and He taught them many lessons for living in His kingdom. One of the most important lessons Jesus taught His disciples was how to pray (see Luke 11:1).

I think it is very important to talk about prayer as being a form of conversation with God. We might sometimes mistakenly think of prayer as the shopping list that we hand God to do helpful, important, and necessary things in our lives and for the world around us. Of course, prayer can be a divine shopping list, but if we do not allow prayer to be a conversation with God, then we will most certainly exclude ourselves from a deeply satisfying intimacy with God. What does Jesus say in response to His disciples' request about learning to pray?

We find Jesus' instructions regarding prayer in two references: Matthew 6:9-13 and Luke 11:2-4. The content in Matthew is more extensive, so we will use that passage for this Conversation Starter. But before we dive into this adventure, let's think about some observations that could be helpful with the Lord's Prayer.

For starters, it is possible that you are familiar with this prayer. It has been used throughout Christian applications, denominations, references, texts, liturgies, songs etc., for millennia. Unfortunately, because it is so commonly used, its mechanical repetition can make it seem inert and irrelevant. The adage, "Familiarity breeds contempt" comes to mind when I think about the Lord's Prayer. We may know it so well that we might neglect to pay attention to its implied invitation to converse with God. I can find myself mindlessly repeating the Lord's Prayer in various church services or liturgical expressions without purposefully being present with what I am saying.

I think it can also create some challenges for us when we treat the Lord's Prayer as a religious relic that is useful to help us feel pious and formal in our religious posture. I have been in church services where the congregational repetition of the Lord's Prayer has seemed formulaic—a version of checking the box. But I also have had wonderful and intimate experiences with God as I have prayed this prayer. I absolutely

HEY GOD, CAN WE TALK?

want to acknowledge that God can and does work in whatever space or context we provide or allow.

How can the Lord's Prayer be a Conversation Starter for us? In the next few pages, I have resourced you with a new perspective and application for Jesus' instructions on prayer for His followers. In this application, we look at prayer from more of a conversational point of view and not strictly from a petition perspective. Before we jump into this adventure, let me share a personal example from conversations I have had with some of my friends.

Over the years I have had many wonderful friends. Some of my friends have been with me in a season when we were going through similar experiences, like raising our kids or pursuing our careers. Some of my friendships have revolved around a common activity, such as a Bible study, a workout group, a common activity like pickleball or softball, or even a cooking club. And I have a few friends whom I cherish because of the longevity of our relationships, regardless of the season of life or what was happening around us. They have been great friends even when the calendar demands might have made us less consistent than we would have chosen. Over the course of various friendships in my life, the ones that I most enjoy and that have the greatest depth are the ones that have had the most consistency and intentionality.

These friendships have relied on consistent conversations. With some of my friends, our conversations can start with questions like, "How did you sleep? Have you heard from your kids? How are you feeling? Did you have a quiet time with God?" Over the course of the conversation with my close friends, we will transition into talking about various experiences, things we want to accomplish for the week, or maybe some emotional struggles or funny encounters. We might also chat about hurtful events, dreams we have in our hearts, stuff that God is talking about with us in prayer, reading the Bible, or a worship experience. In our conversations, we have some steady topics that facilitate the dialogue and serve to deepen our friendship with intentional consistency.

In a similar way, our conversations with God can have some steady topics that can serve as springboards for deeper dialogue and connection. As we look at the Lord's Prayer, I propose that Jesus gives us several springboards or *conversation levers* to help us grow closer to God. Let's look at Jesus' reply when His disciples requested that He teach them to pray:

> *Our Father who is in heaven,*
> *Hallowed be Your name.*
> *Your kingdom come.*
> *Your will be done,*
> *On earth as it is in heaven.*
> *Give us this day our daily bread.*
> *And forgive us our debts, as we also have forgiven our debtors.*
> *And do not lead us into temptation, but deliver us from evil.*
> *For Yours is the kingdom and the power and the glory forever. Amen.*
>
> (Matthew 6:9-13)

As we read through this prayer, I suggest there are eight *conversation levers* that Jesus gives us for conversing with God. In the following paragraphs, I identify each lever and give some ideas about how to facilitate dialogue with God using this conversation lever.

Lever 1:
Our Father who is in heaven,

In this conversation lever, I encourage you to sit with the truth that God is your heavenly Father. To help you do that, here are some questions you could consider:

- In what ways has God been like a father to you?
- In what ways do you see God erroneously based on your earthly father?
- How would God want to father you today?
- How can God be your father in this season in your life?

In this part of your conversation seeing God as your father, you could also take some time to ask for God's help or input about what it might look like to be God's son or daughter. Having ongoing dialogue with your heavenly Father about being His son or daughter can have a very significant impact on your identity and how you see yourself. The potential for rich transformation with this conversation lever is truly magnificent!

Lever 2:
Hallowed be Your name.

With this conversation lever, I have found it helpful to pause and reflect on God being holy.

- What does it mean to be holy?
- How does God express being holy?
- What does God's holiness look like in your daily living?

This lever can also be a place where you can pause to worship and express reverence for God. Sometimes it is helpful to hum a worship tune or listen to worship music. During this time, stop to consider God's creative brilliance, infinite wisdom, unlimited power, unchanging presence, and steadfast loving-kindness—God's glorious character.

In my experience with this conversation lever, I often finish this part with a feeling of deep satisfaction. Maybe that is because worship and reverence is a natural and fitting expression of our relationship with God.

Lever 3:
Your kingdom come.

This conversation lever moves us to a place of acknowledging the sovereignty of God as the King of all kings. This is a fitting space to ask God where His lordship is being compromised or diminished in your life.

- Is God on the throne of your finances, time management, relationships, conversations, thoughts, emotional life, health habits, entertainment choices, sleep habits, and daily routines?

This lever is a great place to invite God's lordship to be displayed through you in genuine love. I encourage you to ask for divine help to sense God's love and to let God love through you. Along those lines, how are the gifts of the Spirit and the fruit of the Spirit being displayed in your life? (See First Corinthians 12 and Galatians 5.)

Lever 4:
Your will be done on earth as it is in heaven.

- What is God's will in heaven?
- How is that translating to your life on earth?
- How would you see God's will being expressed in your daily living?

- In what ways can I participate with God to accomplish His will on earth?

For this conversation lever, position yourself to agree with God's will. We want what is done in heaven to be done on earth. Invite God's will to be accomplished in various decisions, situations, experiences, relationships, priorities, and more in your life.

Because you are made from the earth—God shaped Adam from the dust of the earth—invite God's will to be done in your body. Since there is no sickness in heaven, pray to be healed of any sickness or disease you may have.

Lever 5:
Give us today our daily bread.

With this conversation lever, it is helpful to ask God for daily provisions such as time, energy, wisdom, finances, schedule assistance, or relational connections.

- What will you need for today?
- What is the daily bread that you foresee needing?
- Ask God how He might meet your needs today.

This lever positions you to see God as your Provider. Look to Him for your provision and not to your job, your own efforts, or your own energy. Acknowledge that you cannot rely on your own wisdom or intelligence. Express gratitude for the various areas of provision that God has given to you.

Lever 6:
Forgive us our debts as we forgive our debtors.

In this conversation lever, we take an inventory of our rela-tionships to assess where there might be a need for forgive-ness. Because of the conditional nature of forgiveness that Jesus describes here, this is an extremely important lever. The word *as* tells us that to receive forgiveness, we must choose to forgive.

- Are there people you need to forgive?
- Are there people from whom you need to ask for forgiveness?

When I talk with God with this lever, I will often sense Him speaking to me about someone I need to forgive. This can be about a recent event that happened or about a person who makes me scratchy. The only way I know how to get good at forgiveness is to keep practicing.

With that said, I am not advocating the continuation of an abusive relationship. Forgiveness means we release a per-son from punishment and retribution, but it does not mean we stay in a cycle of abuse or continual pain.

Lever 7:
Do not lead us into temptation, but deliver us from evil.

With this lever, I have found it helpful to ask God to help me identify things that are tempting to me, and then ask why these things are tempting. Upon making these identifications, I ask God to help me stay away from these weak spots and vulnerabilities. I also ask God to deliver me from the plans and devices the evil one would try to use against me.

Here are some questions to consider:

- What things in your life could be weak spots for temptation?
- What would be some beginning steps that could lead you into full-blown temptation?
- Are there areas in your life that might have some evil that you could bring to God for deliverance?

I really appreciate this lever because it reminds me that there is an active enemy seeking to hurt, diminish, and even kill me. This lever also encourages me to keep aligned with God in the battle and to pay attention to the enemy's schemes to deceive, accuse, derail, or condemn.

Lever 8:
Yours is the kingdom and the power and the glory forever.

In this final lever, it is very refreshing and validating to acknowledge the truth and reality that God's kingdom, power, and glory continue forever and ever. There is no end or limit to the glory of God. His power and His lordship are not limited in either time or space.

This lever tells us that God is infinite. We need this steady reminder because we are finite and are living in a limited world. We are bound by revolutions around the sun and the march of time that doesn't stop. God, being infinite, doesn't have our definitions, sequencing, or constraints.

This is a fitting and appropriate way to finish this way or method of conversing with God. In this lever, we can sit with God's omnipresence, omniscience, and omnipotence, inviting all of God to participate in our daily existence. We can also choose to trust in God's character that is loving, all-wise, compassionate, and faithful when we don't see the tangible expression of God's participation in various life events.

I suggest that you set aside some time daily to sit with God in each conversation lever. You might find it helpful to have some paper with you to write down what you sense, or maybe take notes on your phone so that this kind of conversation with God can be portable. I also suggest that you give this Conversation Starter several opportunities over the course of a few months. The Lord's Prayer was Jesus' answer to His disciples' request for learning to pray and converse with God; and it has been my experience that the more opportunities I give for this way of conversing with Him, the richer, deeper, better, and more fulfilling it can be.

For further reflection and note-taking see "Lord's Prayer" on page 240 in the Epilogue.

8

CAN WE TALK—
MY EMOTIONS ARE RAW

How do you talk with someone who is all-knowing? What do you share with someone who is always with you? What do you say to someone who can do anything and is all power-ful? How do you talk with someone who is entirely "other"?

In my travels around the world, I get to talk with people who are totally different from me. I have talked with government leaders, healthcare experts, intellectual heavyweights, children of sex workers, teachers, aid workers, farmers, working mothers, and heaps of different kinds of people. Many of these individuals have massive cultural differences from me. They also have upbringing contrasts, diverse worldview perspectives, and economic disparities. Talking with such a wide range of people is a very interesting experience, and it can be very illuminating in regard to revealing differences in our ways of life, views, and values.

Sometimes I find it difficult to talk with people who are different from me. While talking with people who have similar cultural alignment, educational commonality, and life experiences can be enjoyable, it can also be boring because of the absence of contrast.

When we begin to think about talking with God, let's appreciate that we bring to the conversation our own assumptions or training that can influence how we talk with God. For example, when I was growing up, I had friends from different faith traditions who had a high quality of reverence about talking with God. They also believed that God was distant and disconnected from their lives. When they talked with God, it seemed formal, cold, detached, and obligatory.

Although I can appreciate their desire to be respectful in how they approached God, I think it is unfortunate that they weren't more candid with Him about their lives. It is a shame that they did not expect nor invite God to participate in their lives on a daily level. When I read the book of Psalms or look at David's life from the Old Testament, I see a sharp contrast to a detached, religious, or traditional perspective.

I propose that when we talk with God, we have two main postures—real time and real words.

REAL TIME

What does it look like to talk with God in real time? When we look at David's life, it is very encouraging to read about his real-life existence and not some manufactured ideal to which we can't relate. I appreciate that when Samuel comes to Jesse's household to anoint the next king of Israel, Samuel follows God's direction to anoint David, the youngest brother who was overlooked by his dad. Samuel prays over David to be Israel's next king.

Shortly after this divine selection, we read that David confronts Goliath, the Philistine champion, and defeats him with a slingshot. This action springboards an Israelite victory over their Philistine enemy. On the heels of this victory, David is brought into Saul's inner circle and is asked to play his harp to soothe Saul's soul. Along the way, David became the best friend of Jonathan, Saul's son. From all these incredible developments, it looks like David's life has shifted into smooth sailing and supernatural favor.

Except! Everything goes terribly wrong for David, because Saul becomes jealous of David's successes and favor. Consequently, for the next ten years or so David takes a literal flight for his life. In the midst of this, David writes multiple psalms in real time. In them he describes his fear, angst, frustration, uncertainty, and discouragement.

This reminds me of an experience I had in my early twenties when I was living in China for a summer. At that time, I was a very conservative and intellectual believer in Jesus. I maintained what I thought was a healthy skepticism for anything supernatural or emotionally expressive related to God. I felt that anything supernatural could be rationally explained. This point of view worked for me until I had a very disturbing demonic dream that woke me in the night and almost paralyzed me in fear. In that real-time moment of terror, I shuffled into the brightly lit hallway of the dorm where I was staying so I didn't wake my roommate.

I slid down the wall and crouched on the floor with my Bible, grateful for the comfort of the light and the comfort of reading the Bible. I prayed to ward off the lurking terror dancing in my emotions from the nightmare. In that real-time moment, I leaned into God for any form of comfort and peace, even when it meant stretching past my intellectual and rational comfort zones. God helped me in that moment. It was such a powerful experience that I still feel it even as I write about it now. There is much to be said for conversing with God in our real-time living!

REAL WORDS

While I remember the emotions and peace that God gave me when I was so disturbed by the dream, I did not write down the words of our conversation. Because of that, I cannot remember specifically the words I spoke to Him. In contrast, when David was fighting for his life against the threats of Saul, he wrote down his thoughts. We can see those in several psalms that he wrote. He used real words to describe his real life, his emotions, and his faith in God that was being challenged.

I encourage you to spend some time reading both the events and the accompanying psalms to see David's real-time words to God. In these psalms, you will see a man pouring out his heart to God without religious filters or proper etiquette protocols. David is both real and raw with God during this massively difficult time of his life. Consider the following psalms—real words—that accompany real-time events:

- Michal, David's wife, protects him from Saul in First Samuel 19:11-17; see Psalm 59
- David flees to Gath, a Philistine city, in First Samuel 21:10-15; see Psalms 34 and 56
- David runs to the cave in Adullam in First Samuel 22:1-3; see possibly Psalm 142
- Saul has eighty-five priests and their families killed in First Samuel 22:9-19; see Psalm 52
- The Ziphites tell Saul about David hiding among them in First Samuel 23:19-29; see Psalm 54
- David cuts off a piece of Saul's robe in Engedi in First Samuel 24:1-22; see Psalm 57

After David becomes king of Israel:

- The events of Bathsheba, Uriah, and Nathan the prophet in Second Samuel 12; see Psalm 51
- Absalom tries to take the kingdom from David in Second Samuel 15; see Psalm 3
- David's plans to build the temple in Second Samuel 17; see Psalm 30

When I read what David says in the psalms that corresponds to the real-life events he is living, I see a powerful demonstration of the importance of being vulnerable and real with God. I know this to be true from many personal experiences.

For example, one Sunday shortly before heading out to church, my husband, Reece, got my attention. When he tried to talk to me, his speech was slurred and garbled. I immediately knew something was seriously wrong, and I rushed him to the ER. They diagnosed him as having had a series of strokes, and they flew him by helicopter to an ICU that specialized in strokes. I made sure my kids were okay and on their way to church, and then I unraveled. As my friend drove me to the ICU, we prayed. I poured out my heart to God with abundant tears, nose blowing, and sobbing breaths.

I said something like, "God, please be gracious and look after my husband. Please give the doctors wisdom and put the right people together to care for him. Please help me to have wisdom and strength for whatever situation I enter when I enter the ICU. Please protect and heal whatever has been damaged in Reece's body and brain." My friend also prayed with me as she drove. She was a steady and strong presence to me in this seemingly very long drive.

When we arrived at the ICU, I walked into Reece's room not knowing what to expect. I was trying not to let my mind go down the very dark possibilities that I might have been confronting. I will never forget walking down the sterile hospital hallway asking God, "Please help me to be strong no matter what I see or hear. Please help me to sense You, and please give me wisdom for whatever happens in the upcoming hours and days." God did communicate with me, and He answered my prayers by giving me strength, hope, wisdom, grace, patience, practical support, and lots more.

Reece didn't have any more strokes, was held for testing and observation for twenty-four hours, and then was released to return home. To this day, he has not had another stroke. I am thankful to God for looking after him. I am grateful that God communicated with me in such a variety of ways during this very disturbing crisis. I think this is a powerful, modern example of the reciprocal nature of conversing with God.

Let's continue to look at David and explore one of his real-life experiences. We can look at a psalm that he wrote to see the dialogue between God and David. I want you to notice this, because I have found that conversations with God often don't look the same as conversations that I have with humans. Indeed, it is helpful to think about our conversations with God as we keep in mind two very important factors.

First, in our dialogue with God, we must remember that we are *finite* and have physical limits and time constraints. Our lives move in sequence and maturation. We live an existence of matter and limited space over the course of days, weeks, and years. In contrast, God is infinite and not limited to or controlled by matter or the law of nature. Furthermore, while God made time and blessed it, God exists outside of time (see Genesis 2:3). He is not constrained by sequence, age, deadlines, nor the passage of time in months or millennia. When we communicate with God, we would be wise to remember His infiniteness.

The second important factor to keep in mind when dialoguing with God is that our communication norm is horizontal in nature. By this I mean that the human point of view for conversation and communication is based on engaging with other humans, peer to peer or friend to friend. Even the communication that happens between a parent and a child or a supervisor and an employee is horizontal in nature because it is human to human. In contrast, the communication that happens between God and us is not horizontal in nature. Instead, conversations with God have a vertical nature.

In our communication with God, we need to remember that God is not human, nor confined to the limits of time or space. Talking with God won't always look like talking with another human. In my own experience, I have sensed God communicating with me in many ways that go far beyond a human dialogue. One of the ways that God communicates with me is through impressions that I have. These look like subtle reminders or desires that don't come from my natural inclinations.

Given these observations, let's look at an example in David's life. Let's see what this kind of communication looks like for him and how it could also be relevant in our communication with God. The Bible describes one of David's many real-life experiences when he was running from Saul to save his life:

> *Then David arose and fled that day from Saul, and went to Achish king of Gath. But the servants of Achish said to him, "Is this not David the king*

of the land? Did they not sing of this one as they danced, saying, 'Saul has slain his thousands, and David his ten thousands'?" David took these words to heart and greatly feared Achish king of Gath. So he disguised his sanity before them, and acted insanely in their hands, and scribbled on the doors of the gate, and let his saliva run down into his beard. Then Achish said to his servants, "Behold, you see the man behaving as a madman. Why do you bring him to me? Do I lack madmen, that you have brought this one to act the madman in my presence? Shall this one come into my house?" (1 Samuel 21:10-15)

Based on what we read, it is obvious that David fears for his life and exhibits bizarre behavior in an attempt to save his life. What does communication with and from God look like in this scenario? The answer to this question is found in Psalm 34 where David pours out his heart to God and we can see God indirectly communicating with David:

I will bless the Lord at all times; His praise shall continually be in my mouth. My soul will make its boast in the Lord; the humble will hear it and rejoice. O magnify the Lord with me, and let us exalt His name together (Psalm 34:1-3).

What does God communicate back to David in this psalm? I would suggest to you that God's communication back to David is less explicit and more indirect. Let's look at verses 4-9 to discover what God is communicating with David at this time. Please focus on the content in bold to see what and how God is communicating with David:

> I sought the Lord, and **He answered me, and delivered me** from all my fears. They looked to Him and were **radiant,** and their faces will never be ashamed. This poor man cried, and the Lord **heard him and saved him** out of all his troubles. The angel of the Lord **encamps around** those who fear Him, and **rescues** them. O taste and see that the Lord **is good;** how **blessed** is the man who takes refuge in Him! O fear the Lord, you His saints; for to those who fear Him **there is no want** (Psalm 34:4-9).

When I read the combination of David's real-life events along with the psalm that he wrote to God pertaining to this event, it helps me see the link between my life's experiences and God communicating with me—even when God's communication is less explicit and not very concrete. I think this is important for us to consider, because much of our human or horizontal communication is generally more direct or explicit. God's communication with us doesn't always fit our human paradigms or expectations.

These two factors, finite versus infinite, along with horizontal versus vertical, affect the communication that happens between God and us. As God communicates with us, we would be wise to keep in mind these filters and perspectives so that we can grow in our appreciation of the massive variety of ways that God communicates in our daily living.

When I asked the question on my Facebook page about the ways that God communicates with us, I had more than 110 replies. Of course, some of the replies were the same, but I was very inspired and surprised by the diversity of ways and descriptions of how God communicates with us. The following are some of the replies to my question. Maybe some of these answers will also help you see some new ways or contexts that God communicates with you.

God communicates with us through:

- dreams
- conversations with friends
- strangers
- family experiences
- a sunrise or sunset
- an inner witness
- a worship song
- mistakes or poor decisions
- a prophetic word
- love from a fellow believer
- a miraculous experience
- peace in the soul regardless of circumstances
- listening to a sermon, podcast, or YouTube content
- repetition of a word
- a sense of unexplainable joy
- journal writing

- a beautiful picture
- observing something glorious or incredible in nature
- undeserved forgiveness
- strength to do another difficult or challenging day
- answered prayer
- hugs from a friend or family
- relationship with our kids or parents
- visions
- a quiet impression
- wisdom for a decision

Hopefully this list will give you some fresh ideas about the ways God can communicate with you. Let's also consider, for a moment, that much of how we communicate is responding to God reaching out to communicate with us. I think it is helpful to remember that God has always been the *initiator* throughout the course of human history. God has set into place His plans, promises, and purposes to which we respond. For example, God initiated the process of anointing David to be the king of Israel to replace Saul. As a result, David responded to God's initiative by developing his leadership skills. David also:

- Called on God's help to preserve his life.
- Asked for God's direction in making decisions.
- Encouraged himself in the Lord when the circumstances of his life were abysmal.

- Valued God's anointing on Saul, even though Saul's behavior was atrocious and deadly.

Ultimately, let's appreciate that the love we may feel in our hearts for others, ourselves, or God is a response to God loving us: *"We love, because He first loved us"* (1 John 4:19). I propose to you that all of God's communication and efforts with humanity are grounded in love because God is love (see 1 John 4:8). The ultimate demonstration of God's love for us was expressed when He gave His life for us: *"For God so loved the world, that He gave His only begotten Son, that whoever believes in Him shall not perish, but have eternal life"* (John 3:16).

As we finish this chapter, let's not forget or ignore the importance of how God will use the Bible to communicate with us. This medium of God conversing with us is available for us to experience anytime in our 24/7 existence, and it is the most certain and concrete communication from God that we have. The Bible overflows with timeless wisdom, unchanging truth, encouragement, and helpful insights into God's character and posture toward humanity. We would be wise to let the word of God dwell richly in our hearts (see Colossians 3:16).

TAKEAWAYS

1. Read the rest of Psalm 34 and circle or underline all of God's actions and activities to help you see more ways God can communicate with you.

2. Write your own psalm to respond to the variety of ways that God is communicating with you.

3. Read Job 33:14: *"For God does speak—now one way, now another, though no one perceives it"* (New International Version).

4. Read First Kings 19:12: *"After the earthquake was a fire, but the Lord was not in the fire; and after the fire a sound of a gentle blowing."*

CONVERSATION STARTER: CREATIVITY AS A SPRINGBOARD

My dad was always super creative. He used lots of mediums to express his creativity, including refinishing antique furniture, painting pictures, making up songs, creating an ongoing story about talking skunks, and surprising us with his intriguing and eclectic choices of clothing.

The talking skunk stories, which we affectionately called "Stinky Stories," was my dad in his best self. In these stories (that not only included talking skunks but also eagle transportation and an imaginary trip to Disneyland), my dad's natural creativity was massively entertaining when I was a little girl. His stories almost always included Jesus as an active participant in these fantastical adventures. My childhood imagination was tantalized through my dad's creative storytelling. Just as importantly, I suspect that some of my relational paradigm through which I see Jesus was influenced by these stories.

I think it is helpful to look at my dad's creativity with "Stinky Stories" as a possible platform for experiencing conversations with God. I believe it is truly important to use creativity as the medium for a dialogue with God. And as I think about creativity, it can be really helpful to consider from the outset that God is the Ultimate Creator. We are uniquely made in His image (see Genesis 1:26). I believe that there is a creative bent in each of us, and this bent can be expressed in a variety of contexts. Oftentimes, people assume that creativity is only expressed in the traditional forms of music, painting, sculpting, poetry, or other outlets.

I suggest we consider that creativity can be expressed in a wide array of contexts. Some platforms for creativity that are not quite so obvious can include business solutions, cooking adventures, housecleaning ideas, scrapbooking, creative dance, gardening, time usage and calendar planning, clothing selections, interior decorating, budgeting designs, people configurations for teamwork, and lots more! The point of this Conversation Starter is to introduce to you the possibility that you can have some very amazing conversations with God with creativity as the medium.

I asked some of my creative friends about their conversations with God. Within this group of creative friends from whom I have solicited this input are musicians, painters, photographers, writers, and chefs. As a guide for their input, I sent each of them a questionnaire. I think their answers and insights will be hugely helpful to you and will provide some insightful illumination and application for your own conversations with God.

These are some of the questions I sent to my friends:

1. What is your preferred medium of creative expression or outlet?

2. How has your creativity enhanced your connection and/or intimacy with God?

3. What do you feel when you are creating?

4. How do you distinguish or discern what is for public display or private intimacy?

5. What does that creative expression look like in a daily context?

6. What else would you add for the creative context for conversing with God?

I used these questions as a springboard to explore their unique conversations with God. I discovered some phenomenal wisdom and applications for us. As you read through their answers, I encourage you to think about your own creativity, your preferred mediums for expression, and how your conversations with God can grow in these creative outlets.

How has your creativity enhanced your connection and intimacy with God?

My friends' answers were so profound and insightful. Here is how they answered the question:

I thank God every time I hear a brilliant lyric, a beautiful melody, or a moving rhythm. Music, particularly worship, is such an incredible gift, as it connects people in a way that nothing else can. I love that I can have a completely intimate moment with the Father while I am mixing even in the midst of 1,000 other people who are also simultaneously having similar moments. It also makes me appreciate the silence and being able to listen. So much of what I do involves me listening intently, and that has taught me to just sit and listen to God. **–TD**

I think creativity is a window into the heart of God. It is an aspect of Himself that He shared with us, as His creation, in order to draw us closer to Him. When I tap into creativity, I tap into the heart of God. I am able to catch a glimpse of the beauty and love that God has for me because of the love I have for what I have created. It is unique and specific. Being creative is like opening a gift from God with each experience. Beauty, love, community, inspiration, meaning, and joy—these are all gifts from my Creator that I have experienced through the process of creating. **–GH**

The intuition that makes someone artistically minded is a specific sensitivity to invisible things or truths that are below the surface of life, objects, and events. Artistic talent is the ability to transform or manifest those internal senses into something external or observable, like a painting, poem, or song. When Christ has enlightened this intuitive process with wisdom, it becomes more than a vague sense of beauty. It becomes a lens to seeing God's essence, His patterns, and His love expressed everywhere. This means that I am surrounded by access points to knowing Him more deeply. When I choose to explore or dig deeper into one of these access points through the art-making process, through meditation, or through worship, the result is intimacy. Not just intimacy with God, but also with creation, other people, and myself. This is the ironic thing about focusing your attention on God—you end up seeing everything more clearly.

The Word is also a major key because expressions of God's nature can always be experienced as "conversations of Scripture." This process is where I recall or present Scriptures of affirmation to the manifestation of God that I am seeing, and the manifestation replies with Scriptures in return. This shouldn't come as a surprise, because the Word is the substance of His being. **–DG**

For me, my creativity actually has been enhanced because of my relationship with God. I never felt truly creative until I discovered the gifts that He placed in me. Where I used to gain my value from people benefitting from my creativity, I now get that from God. That makes me want to continue to create, because I sense His pleasure and enjoyment whenever I am creating. **–JH**

Since God was the first Creator, it has helped me to connect with Him on the creative level. In some ways it is like two musicians talking about music, or two CEOs talking about business, or two moms talking about their children. There is a connection. The connection I feel with God is like two artists talking about creativity. Or at least He is mentoring me in creativity. It has really broadened my relationship with God. Rather than just Him being Savior and Lord, I feel we can connect on the creative level. It is much more personal and intimate. **–DR**

Just like every area of life, I usually get into sticky situations while writing music with multiple people. I always lean on God for help on both the good and bad days. –**BW**

> I sense God when I write because there is discovery, acceptance, compassion, patience, wisdom, presence, time, acceptance, attention, and grace. **–SB**

How do you feel when you create?

As you think about the answers given by my friends, I think you can find some unique perspectives that might help you weave together the concepts of creativity and conversing with God. Here are their answers to the question:

> I feel very present when I mix, particularly mixing live sound. Every instant counts, as there is no second-guessing while a performance is happening. The energy from the crowd and the artist is exciting to me, and as the mixing engineer I am given a certain amount of control over that energy through volume, instrument balance, and the overall tone of the mix. There are very few things more satisfying for me than when a worship band is doing a build, the audience has their hands up deep in worship, and right as the band drops the chorus, I push the master fader up by 2dB. The anticipation, the way that this moment hits the audience in the chest, and the impact of that little extra burst of air creates so much more energy and excitement in the room. In a sense, it builds the faith of those in

the room. When people worship, they want to have an experience with God, and I believe that the tools and talents God has given musicians and sound engineers are His way of stewarding those moments and experiences to connect with humans through their senses. **–TD**

Freedom. Creating is the ultimate freedom for me. It allows me to shut off my stress, my anxiety, and my emotional struggles and just be. I can process through what is real and what is fake, and what experiences have truly occurred or what I have built up in my head as false. With that freedom comes immense joy and clarity. **–GH**

It depends, but I would say that my ideal creative state is one where I feel especially attuned to my environment, my thoughts, even the workings of my own body. This heightened "in the moment" sense makes everything I do feel meaningful and important. The movements as I work with my materials and the thoughts that I entertain as I address the canvas or paper helps the process to feel magical or sacred. It is in this place that God and I can meet and exchange ideas and craft together. This way, whatever the result of my work is art-wise, it has been important, effective, and worthwhile. **–DG**

I feel alive and valued when I create. **–JH**

As a painter, I try to paint with emotion and feel emotion as I create. Interestingly enough, whatever a painter is experiencing and feeling will come out in the paint and the image being created. It could be in color choices, paint application, etc. So technically, each painting has a different feeling and emotion because emotions can vary and fluctuate. The key is probably keeping the emotions and feelings in a steady state so that what I am creating is steady and consistent and not all over the place. I don't think I necessarily "feel God overpowering me" and doing the painting for me. It is still me, but I do feel as I commit my hand and eye to Him, He will guide them. I receive His guidance in that area by faith. **–DR**

I usually feel pressure LOL. I have had insecurity issues my whole life, and that usually fuels the creativity. It is like always wanting to prove myself again, but I know it is not healthy LOL. **–BW**

I feel exhale and deep satisfaction, free from criticism or critique, failure, accusation, freedom to explore and process, discovery, answers/solutions, safety, refuge, contentment, fun, excitement, home, and adventure. **–SB**

How do you distinguish what is for public display or private intimacy?

The answers that I received in response to this question were interesting. Many of the folks I interviewed make a living based on their creativity; consequently, a lot of them differentiate their work by recognizing what is profitable and helpful versus what is appealing for an audience. At the same time, each person I interviewed acknowledged, either directly or indirectly, that they need or value private creativity. Every person I interviewed agreed that not everything they create is for public display.

I think this can be helpful to us because it creates a space for intimacy between you and God in the context of your personal creative connection. Giving yourself permission and room to have private creativity can foster greater intimacy and vulnerability in your conversations with Him.

What does that creative expression look like in a daily context?

The answers I received to this question were interesting and spanned a wide spectrum. The following are some answers I think will be helpful to you.

Creative expression is being open to dive into the experience on a daily basis whenever and wherever inspiration strikes. It takes diligence and determination to hone your creativity. I think of my own creativity, specifically writing and creating music, as a muscle. It needs to be strengthened daily. That could be 5 minutes or 5 hours out of my day, but the point is that I am doing it. I am engaging with God and myself while remaining open to going wherever the art wants to go. **–GH**

Currently for me, my creative expression on a daily basis looks like cooking a meal of some sort. **–JH**

Just getting into a room with my bandmates and trying to have fun. Music is a gift from God, and although I struggle with insecurities, I try to remind myself to have fun! **–BW**

I write every day in many contexts: my daily quiet time journal, daily writing for my own voice, and then weekly blogs, sermons, books, articles, etc. **–SB**

What else would you add for the creative context for conversing with God?

One of the neat things about mixing live and being very present, like I mentioned earlier, is that it puts me into almost a meditative state. As I mix, I am very aware of how I feel Holy Spirit moving in the room. That conversation and that engagement directly affects the way that I mix, and I believe the musicians live in that same space. We all work together to flow with Holy Spirit and to take the congregation where we feel God is telling us through dynamically changing the arrangements of songs on the fly and balancing the way everything comes together musically. **–TD**

At the risk of sounding like a Nike ad, just do it! I can't tell you how important it is to flex that muscle. Like many things in life, it is so easy to say no to an experience of creativity. "I'm too busy," "I'm not good enough," or "I don't have the means" are the most common excuses I have heard for not taking the time to create. Everyone is born with the ability to create. It is an innate ability that has been written into our very core. When you shut yourself off from your creative gifts, you deprive yourself from experiencing the uniqueness of God and His specific heart for you. **–GH**

The results of creative, artistic living shouldn't only be poetic and abstract. Having your "head in the clouds" doesn't have to mean that your feet aren't also on the ground. Your life should reflect a deep grounding in reality...but a deeper, more rich reality. Anyone who's life is in disarray or out of order is not living victoriously, regardless of their artistic or spiritual sensibilities. True spirituality isn't ignoring the responsibilities of the physical world, but rather understanding them in their true context and helping others to see that as well. Fretting about money, or politics, or relationships doesn't make your life more real. But by learning the skills of the artistic mind, you can see God's beautiful reality more clearly. Hopefully help others see it more clearly also. **–DG**

Conversation is key to creativity! Conversing with God and others who are like-minded in their creative expression is extremely important. I would also say observation is a good thing because we learn both by seeing and hearing. **–JH**

As I finish this Conversation Starter, I acknowledge that it is very different from the rest of the Conversation Starters we have explored in this book. I think that is a very good thing, because I am convinced that intimate conversations can be organically unpredictable and very creative. Furthermore, I think that creativity can give God the space and freedom to talk and converse with us in wide and open landscapes.

So, what would this look like for you? I suggest that you explore various creative outlets that could be appealing to you. You may already have a sense for what creative outlets are attractive and helpful to you. Or, maybe the idea of exploring creative outlets might be foreign or even intimidating to you. But regardless of your perspective or experience, give yourself permission to explore without criticism or disdain.

Once you begin exploring and trying out various platforms for being creative, pay attention to what you sense, what you might hear in your heart, what is energizing, what is encouraging, and what provides life and light to you. For me, it has been very important to tune out the critical voices that say I am dumb or worthless, that what I make is ugly or pathetic, or that I should quit trying. Additionally, I have found it very helpful to be consistent in practicing creativity as a way of being faithful to having conversations with God.

Ultimately, as I create, it seems to me that God gently and gradually affirms me with great love, attention, care, compassion, nurture, and affirmation. Creativity as a conversation with God has been nothing short of a magnificent adventure for me!

For further reflection and note-taking see "Creative (visual art, music and/or worship, cooking, mixing sound, writing)" on page 242 in the Epilogue.

9

CAN WE TALK—
CONVERSATIONS WHEN WE LEAST EXPECT THEM

"Everybody likes you, Sarah!" This is what my dad told me when I was in elementary school after I told him that I didn't have any friends, and nobody liked me. His words felt hollow to me because they didn't harmonize with my experiences or conversations at recess. Furthermore, I felt more dissonance with my dad's perspective when, after I said that I was interested in archaeology, he told me that I wouldn't like being an archaeologist because the digs were lonely. He assured me that I was a "people person."

As I have matured, I have come to realize that my dad, who was a massive extrovert, didn't see me as an introvert even though that is truly my personality. Thankfully, as our society has become increasingly educated and accepting of different personality types, the struggles I felt as an introvert growing up in an extroverted home have mostly been resolved. On the other side of the coin, I can see how many people with extroverted personalities struggle sometimes with being over-talkers. Gregarious extroverts can have an awkward conversation when they are engaged with the quiet observance of a more introverted personality.

I bring up the topic of introverted and extroverted personalities because we all have distinct personalities that set us apart from others. Some of these personality distinctions include being more emotional, detailed, organized, adventurous, steady, quirky, cautious, or analytical.

Recognizing these various characteristics can help us when we think about having conversations, and recognizing our unique strengths, weaknesses, and personalities can bring vital wisdom and insight into our communication preferences. For example, if we have a rejection mindset, then it is possible that we will enter conversations with the assumption that the other person will reject us. We just might self-fulfill that assumption by our actions, attitudes, and words. Or it is possible that we might see ourselves as the person everyone likes and wants to be around, assuming that our scintillating personality is irresistible. That would also affect how we are perceived.

In this chapter, we look at some personality dynamics and how they roll into our conversations with God. I am all the more excited for this chapter for two unique reasons. The first is that we are looking at two women who have conversations with Jesus. This excites me because everyone we have looked at up to this point have been men. The second reason I am excited for this chapter is because the conversations that these women have happen with Jesus, so we get to see what dialogue looks like between God and humans in the daily expression of human existence. We know that Jesus is God who took on human form to live in our finite experience, complete with birth, death, and resurrection.

> *Although He existed in the form of God,* [He] *did not regard equality with God a thing to be grasped, but emptied Himself, taking the form of a bond-servant, and being made in the likeness of men. Being found in appearance as a man, He humbled Himself by becoming obedient to the point of death, even death on a cross* **(Philippians 2:6-8).**

When Jesus lived on earth, He conversed with people in many ways similar to how we interact. But for the purposes of this chapter, we are going to look at His interactions with two sisters, Martha and Mary. We will take into account their unique personalities so that we can make some helpful correlations with our own personalities. To do so, we will look at three very powerful interactions between Jesus and these sisters.

DINNER WITH JESUS

The first interaction we read about between Jesus, Martha, and Mary is when they invite Jesus to dinner at their house (see Luke 10:38-42). In these few verses, we get an insightful glimpse into the personalities of these women. In verse 39, we read that Mary is sitting at Jesus' feet listening to Him teach. This is really informative when we consider that in this culture and at this time in history women were not usually allowed to interact with men. It was a social taboo with a bright line that separated the genders unless there was a family or marital connection. Furthermore, the separation was more accentuated because, while it was permissible for men to have access to education and training, women were relegated to more domestic functions such as cleaning and cooking.

In contrast to Mary's "inactivity" and learner posture, we read that Martha was busy and distracted with her preparations (see verse 40). Both women were behaving consistently with their personalities, which also has application for us in our modern living.

For example, I have a friend who is a massive achiever and may be similar to Martha. She is in perpetual motion, and she is one of the most productive people I have ever met. On any given day, she has already accomplished five tasks before I have even awakened. I am always impressed with her supreme productivity. It is easy for me to see this friend as a Martha archetype.

In contrast, I have another friend who is more contemplative. It can be easy to think that she is not being productive or achieving much; however, when I talk with her, I am entirely astounded by her wisdom, insights, discernment, depth, and sensitivities. Instead of producing external achievements, this friend produces wisdom that is helpful and constructive to living life at deep levels of intentional and even spiritual engagement. It is easy for me to see this friend as a Mary archetype.

It is helpful to consider the conversation that develops between Martha and Jesus, initially about Mary's inactivity. In Luke 10:40-42, we get to enjoy this dialogue:

> *Martha...came up to Him and said, "Lord, do You not care that my sister has left me to do all the serving alone? Then tell her to help me." But the Lord answered and said to her, "Martha, Martha, you are worried and bothered about so many things; but only one thing is necessary, for Mary has chosen the good part, which shall not be taken away from her."*

In Jesus' answer to Martha, He affirms Mary's decision to sit at His feet in learner mode. He celebrates that she made a good decision to listen and connect rather than to achieve and produce. I suspect that Jesus' answer to Martha caused her to pause and possibly take inventory of her priorities and values. It is likely that she stopped to observe the contrast between Mary's priorities and hers.

For some of us, we deeply appreciate Jesus' affirmation of our reflective nature. We love that Jesus validates our passion for intimacy with Him when we make choices that seem to be nonproductive. At the same time, we live in a world and culture that requires attention and achieving. Most of us have responsibilities and demands that cannot be neglected or ignored. We have carpools to maintain, laundry to wash, dinners to make, a house to clean, homework to do with our kids, deadlines for our job, and more tasks than we want to consider in this moment.

Maybe we have a Mary personality, but we live in a Martha world. Or maybe we have a Martha personality and the rat race is sucking the life out of us. How do Jesus' words have application to our modern ways of life? Do we ignore everything to the point of neglect and delinquency? Or do we keep Jesus as a figurine on the mantlepiece for occasional dusting and attention?

How do we reconcile our busy modern living using Martha's skills while still choosing to sit at Jesus' feet as Mary did? Maybe the best way to navigate what seems to be irreconcilable differences is to *integrate Jesus into our daily living*—to invite Him into our daily living for help, participation, and dialogue together. As we go about our daily activities, we can ask Him to help us be increasingly aware of His presence. From my perspective, when we integrate Jesus into our daily living, He helps us achieve what needs to be done for each day. Integration helps us grow in our connection with Him by paying attention to His presence and participation in the daily grind.

DISAPPOINTMENT WITH JESUS

The next interaction that the sisters have with Jesus is right after their brother died. They were massively disappointed in Him, which I can truly appreciate (see John 11). Mary and Martha had summoned Jesus to come and heal their very sick brother, Lazarus. They were both supremely disappointed with Jesus when their brother died because He didn't come to them in time to heal him. When Jesus finally did show up, it was four days after their brother's death. Lazarus was like literally stone, cold dead. Jesus' arrival was probably like pouring salt into a wound.

I believe that the dialogue recorded with Jesus in this chapter is really helpful, because we all have likely experienced times when we were disappointed in Him. I am sure there have been times when you asked Him for something, and He didn't do what you requested or needed.

I remember a time in my life when I was really disappointed with Jesus because I didn't see Him doing anything. I did not feel His presence, hear His voice, or actively experience His participation and intervention in my life. And this "neglect" happened at a time in my life when I was having very violent dreams and experiencing suicidal thoughts. This happened in the summer between my junior and senior year of college when I was studying in Germany for my bachelor's degree.

I was in a very isolated situation studying at a language institute in a small town. I was far from any family, friends, or support system, and I felt more and more disconnected as each day of the eight weeks went by. This disconnect became increasingly difficult for me, and when I reached out to Jesus in prayer or Bible reading, it seemed that everything was flat and nonresponsive. From my point of view, when I most urgently needed Jesus, He seemed to be MIA.

Maybe Martha and Mary also felt like Jesus was MIA when they needed Him the most—when their brother was sick and dying. In this very intense situation, we can learn a lot as we look at the behaviors and words of Martha and Mary. When Jesus returned to their village after Lazarus' dead body had been interred, each sister had individual interactions with Jesus. These conversations reveal not only their personalities, but also Jesus' ability to interact with them and their unique temperaments.

There is a very powerful conversation that develops with Jesus and Martha as she goes out to meet Him. As you read through the dialogue between Martha and Jesus, consider a few things:

- Martha's posture and disappointment with Jesus
- The rational dialogue between Martha and Jesus
- Martha acknowledging that Jesus is very powerful
- Jesus' reply to Martha's words
- The contrast between what each expected: death prevention with Martha and death reversal (resurrection) with Jesus
- Jesus' revelation to Martha in verse 25: *"I am the resurrection and the life"*

Martha then said to Jesus, "Lord, if You had been here, my brother would not have died. Even now I know that whatever You ask of God, God will give You." Jesus said to her, "Your brother will rise again." Martha said to Him, "I know that he will rise again in the resurrection on the last day." Jesus said to her, "I am the resurrection and the life; he who believes in Me will live even if he dies, and everyone who lives and believes in Me will never die. Do you believe this?" She said to Him, "Yes, Lord; I have believed that You are the Christ, the Son of God, even He who comes into the world" (John 11:21-27).

In this back and forth dialogue between Jesus and Martha, Jesus communicates to Martha who He is in terms of resurrection and life. This is in stark contrast with her brother's death. Sometimes the conversations we have with Jesus will run contrary to what seems to be concrete and real in our daily existence. I suspect that Martha struggled to reconcile her dead brother's body in the grave with Jesus' words about Him being the resurrection.

Have you ever had an experience that seemed to defy what you were hearing from God? As I shared earlier, my husband had a stroke several years back. In the midst of that experience, I was able to observe that what was happening in the physical world was defying what was happening in the spiritual world. I will never forget the immediacy of those moments. I was in full crisis mode, with my friend and I praying desperately, and yet I sensed God's peace and calm. This calm was in contrast to the anxiety and panic that was threatening to swallow my thoughts and feelings.

I felt God's presence settling into my soul with peace and assurance as I walked down the hallway of the hospital's ICU ward. When I found my husband's room, I walked in to find him sitting upright, conversant, and relatively healthy. Over the course of the next twenty-four hours, his vital signs stabilized, and he was released to return home. I encountered God through this experience in new ways that helped me grow in my awareness of His power and peace. It is also

possible that in the same way, Martha grew in her appreciation for who Jesus was as He talked with her about resurrection in the context of Lazarus' death.

While Martha's dialogue with Jesus reflects some of Martha's personality, which is practical and conversant, Mary's
interaction with Jesus also expresses her personality. After
concluding her chat with Jesus, Martha goes to Mary and
tells her that Jesus is in town and is asking after her. When
Mary hears of Jesus' presence, she goes out to meet Him.
Her behavior shows us the difference in personalities of the
two sisters:

> *Therefore, when Mary came where Jesus was, she
> saw Him, and fell at His feet, saying to Him, "Lord,
> if You had been here, my brother would not have
> died." When Jesus therefore saw her weeping,
> and the Jews who came with her also weeping,
> He was deeply moved in spirit and was troubled*
> (John 11:32-33).

It is interesting to notice that both Martha's and Mary's
initial words to Jesus were exactly the same. After these initial words, however, Mary's behavior was very different from
Martha's. While Martha continued in dialogue mode, Mary
was in emotional meltdown mode. She was grieving the loss
of her brother with intense wailing and an outpouring of
tears and dramatic emotional expression. Clearly, Jesus was
deeply moved by the emotions He felt and saw expressed
to Him. Indeed, John 11:35 says, *"Jesus wept."* There are only
a few places where it is recorded that Jesus wept, and it is

noteworthy that He joined with Mary and those around her in the outpouring of emotions.

Maybe your personality aligns more naturally with the emotional outpouring of Mary. Or maybe you resonate better with the verbal, logical way in which Mary connected with Jesus. I think it is really important to recognize and accept that Jesus joined each woman in their unique expression of disappointment and grief. Neither of them had to change to fit into Jesus' paradigm for communication and connection. Jesus had a powerful dialogue with Martha. And Jesus had a powerful emotional experience with Mary. Both personalities and expressions were equally valid. Regardless of your personality, you do not need to change to be able to dialogue and experience Jesus.

This insight has been really powerful for me to absorb. There have been several occasions in the past when I have belittled and dismissed my own personality. For quite a while, I looked around at others, observed how they interacted with Jesus, and ended up wanting to be someone I am not. I was impressed by others' wisdom, how Jesus ministered through them, or how intelligent they were in regard to their ability to read and understand the Bible.

Indirectly, I was minimizing my personality by wanting to experience Jesus in the ways I saw others interfacing with Him. While it has taken some time and healthy adjustments, I am now very grateful for who I am and how God has made my unique personality. Some things that have helped me along this journey include various personality tests, conversations with authentic and compassionate friends, counseling, some helpful books, and most of all, Holy Spirit leading me into truth a day at a time.

The final conversation in which we see Jesus interacting with Martha and Mary is found immediately after Jesus raises their brother, Lazarus, from the dead: *"So they made Him a supper there, and Martha was serving; but Lazarus was one of those reclining at the table with Him"* (John 12:2). I want to point out that Martha is still serving while Lazarus is sitting next to Jesus. I make this observation because it shows us that Martha continues to be true to her personality and divine blueprint. She is so practical! When we first meet her, she is concerned about hosting Jesus well. And when she is talking to Jesus about Lazarus' death, she tells Him that Lazarus' body is going to stink since he has been dead for four days. (I always chuckle when I read her practical input to this situation.) And again, in this passage, we see Martha being practical by looking after the commonsense necessities that feeding and hosting Jesus requires.

When we look at Mary, we see that she also remains true to her form. She expresses her connection with Jesus in a more emotional context: *"Mary then took a pound of very costly perfume of pure nard, and anointed the feet of Jesus and wiped His feet with her hair; and the house was filled with the fragrance of the perfume"* (John 12:3). Mary's actions express a very deep emotional connection with Jesus. This is seen not only as she pours out costly perfume, but also in her extravagant expression of love by washing and drying His feet with her hair. In this demonstration of opulent love, we see that Mary is "all in" and is withholding nothing.

This is a really powerful demonstration from Mary upon which we would be wise to pause for consideration. We will go through both mountaintops and valley troughs throughout our lives as we walk with Jesus. A valley trough that Mary experienced was the death of her brother. She desperately wanted Jesus to heal Lazarus so that he wouldn't die, but that is not what happened.

And in our walk with Jesus, it is important to accept that we could be disappointed with Him from time to time when He does not do what we want or pray for. Nevertheless, let's learn from Mary to stay faithful to Jesus and to let go of disappointment so that our love for Him exceeds our expectations of His power, intervention, or provision. Let's be careful not to hold onto our emotions more than we hold onto Jesus.

As we come to the end of this chapter, I ask you to consider a few things from Martha and Mary that might relate to you and your personality. In general terms, most of us either feel an affinity with Martha or an affinity with Mary. Some of us are high achievers, massively practical, and dialed into the demands of our daily living. We get stuff done and sometimes revel in our productivity. In contrast, some of us find a greater affinity with Mary. We have a more emotional approach to life and are not quite as practical as Martha. For those of us who feel greater alignment with Mary, we often experience life through our emotions before we stop to consider what is practical or productive.

Our personalities play an integral part in how we dialogue with Jesus. And to this end, our personalities are to be celebrated because of God's craftsmanship in knitting us together. This is extremely important, because God tells us, *"I will give thanks to You, for I am fearfully and wonderfully made; wonderful are Your works, and my soul knows it very well"* (Psalm 139:14).

You are fearfully and wonderfully made by the Creator of the universe. You are not a mistake, nor is your personality a liability. The way that God has knit you together is to be celebrated and not merely tolerated. You are not like other people, and that is very wonderful! If your personality is more like Martha, please do not try to be Mary. If your personality is more like Mary, please do not try to be Martha. If you are like neither of these women, then please do not try to squeeze yourself into a personality type that is not consistent with the divine blueprint God has made in you.

In conclusion, I pray the end of Psalm 139:14 for you: *"Your soul knows very well"* that you are fearfully and wonderfully made, and not just with mental assent or agreement, but rather to the core of your being! Your personality is a divine gift, and it is important for you to accept and celebrate who you are as a unique person and how your personality is expressed when you are conversing with God!

QUESTIONS FOR REFLECTION

1. Think of a time in your life when you wanted to be somebody other than who you are. How did that season affect your interaction with God?

2. What might God be saying to you about your unique personality?

3. What are the strengths and weaknesses of your personality as you think about conversing with God?

4. How might God celebrate the strengths of your personality?

5. How might God augment or strengthen the weaknesses of your personality?

6. Consider taking a few minutes to ask God to help your soul know very well that you are fearfully and wonderfully made.

CONVERSATION STARTER:
LECTIO DIVINA

I love this Conversation Starter, full stop. It is possible that just maybe it is my favorite one in this entire book. I like it because it is so deeply anchored in the Bible, and I find its application into my daily life *opulent* and *surprising*. It is *opulent* because I find God frequently speaking to me throughout my day about the lessons that I have settled into through this Conversation Starter. It is *surprising* because, when I least expect to experience the Bible, I do.

I find that this happens at random times, such as when I am listening to my husband tell me the same story for the third time, when I am frustrated with one of my teenage kids who is being snarky, when I am waiting for a delayed airplane, or when I have a dream about a Bible passage. In these moments and experiences, I am often surprised by what I sense in my soul. I am reminded of various Bible verses that I have used with *Lectio Divina,* and I allow these verses to come alive in these normal life experiences. I am abundantly giddy to share this Conversation Starter with you and eager for you to try it for yourself. Go through the steps several times to see if you enjoy the glorious adventure that comes with *Lectio Divina!*

The term *Lectio Divina* comes from Latin and means "sacred or divine reading." Rather than reading the Bible for information, obligation, or religious ceremony, we are to come to the Bible from a place of desiring relationship and connection with God. In terms of conversing with God, *Lectio Divina* opens great possibilities for letting Him frame both the topic and the experience of a conversation. This way of conversing with God can be fully transformational as well as richly satisfying!

For some brief historical background, *Lectio Divina* loosely began with Origen, a church father in the third century.[1] It became more formalized with Benedict of Nursia in the sixth century and was firmly established with a Carthusian Monk, named Guigo, in the twelfth century. It has been practiced by Christians for more than a millennium across a wide spectrum of Christian expressions and denominations. The monk, Guigo, established four steps to this conversation, but I have found it helpful to include two more steps to acknowledge and navigate our modern lifestyle. The six steps for this conversation go along this outline:

1. Relax and attend (*silencio*) – to be quiet or silent

2. Read (*lectio*) – to read or absorb

3. Reflect (*meditatio*) – to meditate

4. Respond (*oratio*) – to reply (pray)

5. Rest (*contemplatio*) – to contemplate

6. Try it on (*incarnatio*) – to become incarnate

Let's look at these steps with brief descriptions for each. After this overview, I will walk you through a sample conversation with God using *Lectio Divina* and then suggest some passages you could explore to grow in this style of conversing with Him. If you would like to deep-dive into this style of conversation, I suggest reading Jan Johnson's work, *Meeting God in Scripture*. In the meantime, here is a brief primer to get you started.

Once a passage of the Bible has been chosen, you may begin with **relaxing and attending**. (At the end of this Conversation Starter, I give you a helpful list of possible passages you could chose for dialoguing with God.) This is an essential beginning to all of the conversations we have. Our lives are overflowing with distractions, demands, responsibilities, crises, and the unexpected. Have you noticed that whenever your attention is distracted or fragmented that your conversations become shallow and short? On the other side, our deeper and more fulfilling conversations happen when we exhale and settle into being present—when we are attentive to the other person. This is like sitting down with a friend over a cup of coffee to purposefully be together and to enjoy each other's company.

After spending some time in the first step, our next step is to **read** whatever Bible passage has been selected. In this step, take time to read the Bible passage a few times. For me, usually the first time I read a passage it is kind of a quick jaunt through the words. But when I think of conversing with God around a Bible passage, I take more time and read the passage more slowly. It is helpful to read it aloud so that my ears and my mouth participate in the conversation.

I also suggest that reading a passage several times can help us see and experience things that we do not often catch during a one-time reading. I find the principle of repetition, or echo, a very significant method that God uses in conversing with us. For example, it is not uncommon for me to read something from the Bible in my daily quiet time and then see or hear the same content on a Facebook post, to hear the same thing in a conversation with a friend, to listen to my kids tell me something similar from their day at school, to read the same thing in a book, or to hear the same thing in a podcast during that day. There is much to be said for the value of repetition, and I suggest that repetition helps refine and sharpen our focus, particularly when our existence is dominated with distractions.

After reading the Bible passage slowly and aloud several times, the next part of the conversation with God is to *reflect* on what you are reading. If the passage we are reading is a narrative selection, we get to imagine ourselves in the passage. It can be very helpful to imagine yourself in the scene with the sun warming your face, wearing sandals, maybe smelling the salt in the air from the Sea of Galilee or the fish residue from the nearby boats or nets. Maybe you are sitting and listening. Maybe you are drawing water. Maybe you are helping as a nearby servant. Maybe you are the person with whom Jesus is speaking in the passage. How do you feel? What are your thoughts? What are your impressions and how does the exchange or experience affect you? When you reflect on the passage or imagine yourself in the scene, what might God be helping you to hear, feel, be aware of or experience?

If the passage you are reading is more theological in nature, like something from one of Paul's epistles, then you will pay attention to what stands out to you. You will look for what catches your attention or what glimmers or gets louder. As you reflect on the passage, what seems magnetic to you? What attracts your focus or seems a little brighter? What might you feel or what impression comes as you pause and reflect?

Having taken some intentional time to reflect on the passage and to be attentive to God's participation with you through that passage, the next part of this conversation is to *respond* to what you feel, experience, or notice in the passage. Responding can be expressing gratitude, being in awe of the impression, worshiping in God's presence, repenting for a decision or action that God identified to be displeasing, reveling in God's unchanging love for you, or acknowledging something new that God is showing you. Sometimes my response to God is a question, sometimes I am angry with God about what I have read, or sometimes I am perplexed with God's decisions or actions in the passage I have read.

No matter what, when I respond to God, I am authentic. My responses aren't religious, they are not calibrated for a pious obligation, and they are not scripted by a liturgical reply. Sometimes my responses are messy, emotional outbursts with raw vocabulary and ugly candor. Often times they reflect curious inquiry as I seek to understand or reconcile what I have read within the context of my daily living. Regardless of the reply, responding is an integral part of a conversation. It is possible that God values our response, much as we desire a reciprocal conversation and not just a monologue or a silent presence. Let's remember that our dialogue with God is not always going to be glorious, delicate, pretty, politically correct, refined, polished, or rational. As such, there is much to be said for the value of honest dialogue. It helps us grow closer with God.

After responding to what we have read and experienced, the next step for *Lectio Divina* is to **rest** or pause with the interaction. This is a very important step that shouldn't be ignored or diminished. Indeed, it is very tempting to quit the conversation once we have responded or expressed ourselves. But let's be aware that our conversation isn't finished just because we have communicated our thoughts and feelings. In fact, it has been my experience that after I have expressed myself, if I take some time to pause, I sense God talking with me in response to my words or expressions.

This is the nature of dialogue. I find that the Bible passage with *Lectio Divina* can be a launching pad for some richly fulfilling interaction with God. As with any form of communication with God, the purpose of *Lectio Divina* is to grow increasingly closer and more intimate with God. Taking a pause after we respond gives space for Him to participate in the conversation.

In the final step for *Lectio Divina*, we **try on** an application from the dialogue we have just experienced with God. Sometimes in the **rest** part of the *lectio* adventure, you might hear or sense some application ideas. These might be suggestions from God about how the passage might be applicable in your day, or He might share with you an exercise to practice over some days or weeks. This is the place in the conversation where you can explore with God some creative applications or divine takeaways that make the Bible passage come alive for you. I like this part because it is like taking the conversation I have just had with God and letting it roll into my earthy existence. This is an adventure, and I always like adventures with God—almost as much as I like conversations with God!

As we finish this Conversation Starter, I list several passages for you to explore with God. Also remember that you can find your own passages for *Lectio Divina* with a few helpful suggestions:

1. Try to keep the passage limited to twenty verses.
2. Keep a passage a sequence of verses, not a shotgun smattering over several chapters or books of the Bible.
3. Use a version of the Bible that is accessible for dialoguing. Sometimes stiff language can distract from meaningful dialogue.
4. Give time for the conversation and allow the dialogue with God to continue into the activities and events of your day.
5. Consider doing *Lectio Divina* in a small group and then discussing among yourselves your individual conversations with God.
6. Be diverse with the lectio. Make sure the passages you choose vacillate between the narrative and theological styles of passages.
7. Don't get discouraged if or when a passage is not a spectacular conversation with God. Be steady and celebrate the process and journey.

IDEAS FOR *LECTIO DIVINA* PASSAGES

- Jesus living in us: Ephesians 2:13-22
- Who is our neighbor: Luke 10:25-37
- Hearing God when life is discouraging: 1 Kings 19:3-18
- Fearfully and wonderfully made: Psalm 139:1-16
- When we fail: Matthew 14:22-33
- Wrestling with God: Genesis 32:24-32
- God loves you: Isaiah 43:1-7
- Changed identity: Luke 8:26-39
- Knowing God: Exodus 33:7-16
- What is important: Luke 10:38-42
- Love with action: James 1:19-27
- Spirit-led living: Romans 8:5-17
- God hears you: Mark 5:24-34
- Being God's sheep: Psalm 23
- Be courageous: Joshua 1:1-9

For further reflection and note-taking see "Lectio Divina" on page 244 in the Epilogue.

ENDNOTE

1. *Lectio Divina,* Wikipedia, https://en.wikipedia.org/wiki/Lectio_Divina; accessed May 12, 2020.

10

CAN WE TALK—
CONVERSATIONS THAT FOREVER CHANGE US

As I think back, I have had many conversations that have changed my life. I will never forget the conversation with Terry when he suggested that God might have something other than just teaching the Bible as a plan for my life. That conversation was the beginning of my journey with Saving Moses, the non-profit organization God has designed to look after babies and toddlers with urgent survival needs in developing countries.

I will never forget the last conversation I had with my dad the afternoon before he died. Maybe the word "conversation" would be too generous of a word to describe me sitting next to his bedside and holding his hand as he slipped slowly away from his earthly existence. I will never forget the conversation my daughter had with me when she explained that I was being manipulative by not communicating and giving her the "silent treatment."

I suspect that you have had your share of memorable conversations over the course of your life. These might include conversations with a coach who influenced your pursuit of a sport, or a teacher who stoked your passion for a particular educational interest. Or maybe you had a conversation in a Bible study, a book club, or a small group that helped you experience God in ways you would never have dreamed possible. It is interesting to consider how some conversations can be so massively transformational.

And when I think about the conversations Jesus had with various individuals in the Gospels, it is obvious that some of these conversations transformed their lives completely. I think of Jesus' brief conversation with Zacchaeus, the very short tax collector who became generous after talking with Jesus (see Luke 19). Or I think about Jesus' conversation with the woman who the Pharisees caught in adultery and who was paraded in front of Jesus. He told her that He didn't condemn her and that she could go freely and not live in sin any longer (see John 8).

Another incredibly powerful example is the Samaritan woman at the well (see John 4). The conversation that developed between Jesus and this woman never fails to rivet my attention. Indeed, every time I read through their dialogue, I make new observations, sense God's genuine love, appreciate the frailty of this Samaritan woman, and marvel at Jesus' gentle words and clear revelation.

The whole conversation with Jesus starts because He is tired from His journey and sits beside a water well. The Samaritan woman comes to draw water from the well around noon. This was a peculiar time of the day to come draw water because it was a time when no one was usually there. On top of that, when Jesus asks her for a drink of water, He is breaking the norm of the day that dictated that a Jewish man should not talk with a Samaritan woman. This is all highly unconventional. She is not just a little flustered in her reply to His request: *"How is it that You, being a Jew, ask me for a drink since I am a Samaritan woman?"* (John 4:9). And so begins the conversation that will revolutionize this woman's life.

I don't think, however, that she had any sense of this outcome when she asked Jesus this question. Indeed, her question simply reflects the customary curiosity that would naturally have been at the top of her mind. She was making observations about how His behavior ran against the cultural norms for gender relationships. Besides that, the ethnic conflict between Jews and Samaritans made even the most casual interaction—like Jesus' request for water—unthinkable. Thankfully, Jesus bridges these gaps and overcomes the various obstacles.

I am so deeply grateful that Jesus continues to bridge the chasms that would separate us from meaningful dialogue with Him! I have had my share of watching Jesus bridge my chasms and overcome my obstacles to talk with me. Some of these hindrances for conversations with Jesus have included intellectual arrogance that dismissed His input, personal achievements at the expense of intimate engagement with

Him, and hobby distractions that include basketball, movies, and exercise. I think each of us have our own impediments that could derail a meaningful conversation with Jesus. Thankfully, He can overcome these gaps!

And I appreciate all the more that Jesus did not curtly dismiss this woman or ignore her question. In fact, instead of disregarding her question, Jesus provokes further engagement with her by throwing out an intriguing reply, *"If you knew the gift of God, and who it is who says to you, 'Give Me a drink,' you would have asked Him, and He would have given you living water"* (John 4:10).

What is *"living water"*? Furthermore, what does Jesus mean when He brings up the random statement, *"gift of God"*? His way of answering her question about the ethnicity and gender obstacles provokes even more curiosity and engagement from her, illustrated by her reply, *"Sir, You have nothing to draw with and the well is deep; where then do You get that living water?"* (John 4:11).

I like that she is still focused on getting Him some water. I can imagine that she is focusing on the practicality of getting water as a way to distract attention from her less than "normal" relational history. She has a very concrete perspective on His words. Maybe she looked down the well to remember how deep it was. Maybe she was thinking, *What the heck is living water? Where does it come from and how do you get it?* One answer from Jesus leads to more questions from the Samaritan woman.

I think it is important to bring curiosity to your awareness. In this scenario, it is the continuous catalyst for the conversation that deepens and unfolds between Jesus and this woman. And maybe we would be wise to think about this same schematic in our lives. Do we have questions we need to bring to Jesus? What areas in our lives have strange or unexplainable things going on?

It is helpful to look at how Jesus answered this woman's questions, because He doesn't always explicitly or overtly answer our questions. Maybe the way that Jesus answers our questions is His invitation for a deeper dialogue, richer conversations, and a more intimate connection with us. That is how I see the conversation unfolding between Him and this woman.

I have seen this to be true in my life as well. In my early twenties, for example, I experienced several months when it felt like God had abandoned me. I could not feel God, reading the Bible felt wooden and cold, my prayers seemed hollow and ignored, and I couldn't see God's fingerprints anywhere in my life. Several years later, having survived this wasteland experience, I had this unresolved question that nagged at me. "Where was God during that very dry period?"

I brought this question to Him for quite some time until He finally spoke to me about it. He talked to me about how I had placed my faith in my feelings and experiences rather than placing my faith in God's Word. His Word says that He will never leave nor forsake me (see Deuteronomy 31:6). My curiosity and continued questioning led me to know God more deeply, and the answer that He gave me helped to strengthen my confidence and trust in Him.

Jesus continues His conversation with the woman by telling her, *"Everyone who drinks of this water will thirst again;*

but whoever drinks of the water that I will give him shall never thirst; but the water that I will give him will become in him a well of water springing up to eternal life" (John 4:13-14). As I read about how Jesus talks with this Samaritan woman, His responses evoke curiosity in me. I can only assume it did for her as well. She replies, *"Sir, give me this water, so I will not be thirsty nor come all the way here to draw"* (verse 15).

All of this lovely and curious dialogue comes to an abrupt halt when Jesus tells her to go call her husband. Her curt reply should catch our attention. Her four words, *"I have no husband"* display marked brevity, which is in stark contrast to the conversational tone that had been happening between the two of them up to this point (verse 17).

This reminds me of how I have responded in various conversations when someone asks me about a tender subject. I can be really relaxed and talkative in a conversation about the snow conditions in the mountains for snowboarding, about the rankings of various college basketball teams, or about various ingredients used in cooking a new recipe; however, if a person asks me about a subject that is tender in my heart, like the emotions I felt when my daughter left for college, my words become few because of the intensity of emotion that I feel.

Maybe the Samaritan woman had a similar reaction. Jesus does not tiptoe around the elephant in the room; instead, He jumps smack into the middle of this very tender subject with her, *"You have correctly said, 'I have no husband'; for you have had five husbands, and the one whom you now have is not your husband; this you have said truly"* (John 4:17-18).

I suspect that our Samaritan woman dropped her dentures at this point, if she had dentures. Here is a complete stranger with whom she has only had a brief exchange, and now He is likely exposing the most painful thing in her soul—her inability to stay married and have a lasting and constructive intimate relationship. Remember, on top of talking with a stranger, He is a man and a Jew. If you sit with this for a few minutes, it will become very clear that she might not be comfortable talking about her marital disasters with Him.

She changes the subject, deflecting to topics that could be really interesting to a Jewish man—religion, worship, tradition, and Jerusalem (see verse 20). Anything to avoid the possibly hurtful subject of her multiple failed marriages. Jesus allows her to redirect the conversation and replies with a brief description about how worship works. I, for one, am very touched that Jesus doesn't force her to continue talking about her painful subject. He allows her to talk about a topic that is less tender and personal.

Jesus adds illumination and revelation on the subject of worship, *"But an hour is coming, and now is, when the true worshipers will worship the Father in spirit and truth; for such people the Father seeks to be His worshipers. God is spirit, and those who worship Him must worship in spirit and truth"* (John 4:23-24). It is obvious that He is comfortable telling her even more than what she thought she already knew.

I find that my conversations with Jesus can often show or reveal to me more than what I think I know or understand. For example, I remember talking with Jesus about a person at my kids' school who was really difficult for me to communicate with. When I would talk with this person, I felt as if I was talking with a Martian. I always had to ask her to explain what she was saying, and I would often leave a conversation being sure that she thought I was a moron.

When I prayed about this, Jesus helped me to see behind this person's manicured veneer and cerebral vocabulary. Instead, I was able to observe a scared and insecure person who was hiding in a carefully dressed Kevlar disguise. My conversation with Jesus cleared away the subterfuge and helped me be able to interact with this person with more grace and wisdom. What I thought I knew about this woman, Jesus helped to clarify for me so that my interactions with her became smoother and more gracious. I am very grateful that conversations with Jesus can help us understand things more clearly!

In Jesus' conversation with the Samaritan woman, the dialogue had been about her deepest pain, Jesus' ability to know her deeply, His living water introduction, and the proper location and etiquette for worshiping God. At this point, the woman says, *"I know that Messiah is coming (He who is called Christ); when that One comes, He will declare all things to us"* (John 4:25). It seems that this topic is her way of staying away from the "five-husband-bruise."

Jesus' answer to this statement is nothing less than breathtaking! Jesus tells this woman who He really is, *"I who speak to you am He"* (verse 26). I find Jesus' answer to be altogether spectacular! In this conversation, Jesus not only reveals this woman's deepest hurt and maybe her darkest secret, but He also tells her what His core identity is. This revelation makes this conversation have mutuality and shared intimacy.

It is obvious by the woman's response that she is flummoxed from the revelation that Jesus, the stranger with whom she's been conversing, is the Messiah who had been prophesied for a few thousand years (John 4:28). She leaves her waterpot at the well and heads back to her city. She goes to tell the men, some of whom might have been one of her five husbands, *"Come, see a man who told me all the things that I have done; this is not the Christ, is it?"* (verse 29). Her city responds by going out to meet Jesus. He talked with them about His identity, and they ask Him to stay longer. After spending these days in His presence, the city believes in Jesus as the Savior of the world. And all of this started with Jesus asking a Samaritan woman for a drink of water.

As we have journeyed together through this incredible conversation between Jesus and the Samaritan woman, we have experienced it in the same sequence in which it occurs in John 4. But I would like for us to consider this conversation from a different vantage point. I believe doing so could be extremely powerful.

I would like for you to put yourself in the sandals of this woman. At face value, the progression of the conversation is powerful and riveting. But if we think about it with some time and reflection, it can become all the more powerful. Let's recall that Jesus knows everything. He knew when He sat down by the well how this whole conversation would play out. I think that maybe this Samaritan woman paused to reflect as well.

Maybe these were some of the woman's thoughts: *This man, who ultimately reveals to me His core and true identity, already knew who I was before He initiated the conversation by asking to get a drink of water. And as He kept talking with me, He didn't shut down the conversation. He actually made it more enticing and appealing to me. Furthermore, He knew when He asked for a drink that I had experienced multiple failed marriages. Yet this didn't stop Him from talking with me. And even knowing the very depths of my dysfunction, pain and brokenness, He chose to converse with me. He was not repelled by my failures and shortcomings. I didn't need to pretend to be anyone different with Him than who I really am, because He accepted me. He knew my core self, and He took the risk to reveal His core self to me, which bridged the intimacy connection. I couldn't help but return to my city, lit up with enthusiasm, to bring them to Jesus, who I would come to know and trust through this deep, heartfelt, and transformational conversation!*

I bring these possible thoughts to your attention because maybe you have found it difficult to converse with Jesus in vulnerable transparency. Maybe the failures in your past, your present dysfunctions, or your compensatory Kevlar that protects you from hurting and detaches you from true relationships keeps you from deeply connecting with God. I believe it is possible that if you see the example of this Samaritan woman, you might find some encouragement from her conversation with Jesus.

I suspect that each of us have enough skeletons in our closets and hurts in our hearts to justify the insulated detachment that might keep us at a distance from Jesus. And yet, I know that He would like to sit down with you somewhere common in your life—like the water well for the Samaritan woman—and have a deep and redeeming conversation with you. And maybe Jesus' conversation with you would be longer and more continuous than the relatively brief dialogue between Jesus and this woman. Maybe Jesus would like to talk with you daily over some weeks, months, and years, so that He can cultivate and nourish you in a life that is overflowing with redemption.

As we finish this chapter, I invite you consider joining Jesus in a conversation that explores your heart as well as His identity. There is no shame, no pain, no experience, no dysfunction, and no brokenness that Jesus is unable to heal, redeem, transform, and resurrect. Please accept Jesus' invitation to have a deep and meaningful dialogue with you, regardless of where He might lead the conversation.

QUESTIONS FOR REFLECTION

1. Where might be a "water well" in your life that Jesus might be waiting for a conversation with you?

2. What might be some obstacles you have that would hinder a conversation with Jesus?

3. What tender spot in your heart might Jesus want to talk about with you?

CONVERSATION STARTER:
INTENTIONAL TIME

I am hopeful that you have tried some of the Conversation Starters, or at least considered one to explore and practice. In full disclosure, with this Conversation Starter, I am inviting you to try an experiment. An experiment may sound like an exciting adventure. Or, being part of an experiment may sound like a lab rat undergoing a clinical evaluation, which is not very appealing. This experiment, regardless of your perspective, comes from looking at an American missionary who lived in the Philippines for more than twenty years, Frank Laubach.

Mr. Laubach is most well-known for his work in international literacy. He is the founder of Laubach Literacy International. LLI merged with another organization to form an international literacy organization that is today known as Proliteracy.[1] Since the beginning in 1955, the work of Frank Laubach, and now Proliteracy, has worked in more than one hundred countries and assisted millions of people worldwide in learning to read.

While I heartily applaud Laubach's lasting literacy contribution, I am deeply inspired and intrigued by an experiment he tried for a few years in the early 1930s when he was a missionary to the Moro people in the Philippines. In this experiment, Laubach created what is known as "The Game with Minutes." In this "game," Laubach endeavored to remember God at least once a minute over the course of an hour, cultivating a habit to let his focus instinctively return to Jesus.[2]

He wrote about this experiment in the book titled *Letters by a Modern Mystic.*

Reading Laubach's book is both inspiring and daunting to me, so I decided to try my own version of his experiment, "The Game with Minutes." Instead of doing the minute by minute awareness of Jesus over the course of an hour, I decided to use time as a context for conversing with God. In the next few paragraphs, I describe how to do this experiment. I would love for you to give it a try. In addition, I invited loads of people to join me in this experiment, and I have included some of their feedback to compel and inspire you to try this adventure.

If you have ever read Brother Lawrence's book, *Practicing the Presence of God*, you will find a few overlapping ideas with this experiment. If you have never read Brother Lawrence's book, you might find it engaging and challenging. He writes about the importance of making conversation with God a lifestyle.

I can appreciate that most of the previous Conversation Starters I wrote about are generally more grounded in historical practice and biblical underpinnings; however, I think there is tremendous value and vibrant life potential in this experience. I believe so strongly in it that I have saved it for last. I believe it could possibly have some tremendous relevant help for you in our modern existence where we are prone to distraction, interruption, time drains, and endless responsibilities. I invite and welcome you to join this Conversation Starter!

Here is the experiment:

Give God three minutes of undivided attention four times a day for two weeks.

What: Three minutes, four times a day (morning, noon, afternoon, and bedtime), the same times every day for two weeks.

In those three minutes, the following are some possible options:

- Requests to God
- Give cares and/or worries to God
- Full focus on God (listen)
- Ask for help with distractions
- Worship and glorify God
- Gratitude
- Inventory preceding hours for God's fingerprints
- Vulnerability—give God unrestricted access to emotions, desires, and assumptions

How would God converse with us? Suggestions:

- Resetting focus
- Giving comfort and consolation
- Giving input
- Directing observation
- Questioning perspective
- Sharing fresh point of view

What I suggest:

• Document at least once a day what is happening during the experiment. How do you feel? What do you experience? Frustrations? Benefits? Document the cumulative effect of the experiment.

To get a feel for some of the results and feedback from this experiment, I have listed what various individuals have said and a brief description of who they are. That way you can consider their daily context in light of their observations.

Holly is top-level executive for multimillion-dollar company who is married with two children in college. She is a passionate Jesus lover and a high achiever. She writes:

> The first couple days was fun in that something new for the day popped in each of the four times. Those times were mostly different forms of praise or thanks. I found myself going deep into things I had not thought to praise Him for. After a couple days, I found myself wanting more structure. I prayed about it, and I felt led to do praise and thanksgiving for the first and the last sessions and to leave the middle two times open for the other options with Holy Spirit. I really liked the experiment because it seemed to raise my level of awareness of Holy Spirit—even when it wasn't one of my four times. At times I wished the exercise was longer (more than a few minutes) because

> it was hard to get into it in a short time. By the time I quieted my mind, the time was over. But at other times it was instant submersion and I loved it. All in all, it was a valuable 2-week experiment.

Frank is a professional who is married with two grown children. He writes:

> I must admit that I was initially resistant toward this direction, but it has turned out to be an energizing infusion of freshness in my relationship with Him. I am currently seeing my life in an intensifying season of convergence. Finding an enhanced level of input from the Spirit is perhaps more vital than I even realized. I was thinking my entire life is dependent on Him already!

Claire is a domestic engineer who is looking after two children under the age of five. These are her experiences with this experiment:

> Honestly, I was not faithful every day. However, when I did do it, God showed me a couple things. First, He showed me how much He cares for people. I was out and about when one alarm went off. I looked around and started praying for those around me, and I just got a different perspective.

> He cares so deeply for people. Another, He is not boring! Haha. One of the biggest takeaways is how much I want more of Him. I'm not sure if the two weeks are over, but this exercise has made me more aware of God in the day to day.

Jerome is an engineering student in his early twenties, working to earn his degree in mechanical engineering. He writes:

> I like the idea of four times a day and not one big lump time, as it requires one to continually focus on God. I feel that it is structured well and is a good experiment.
>
> Observations: I didn't really have any profound moments during the experiment. I will admit, I struggled getting the fourth time in. I could always get three times a day in, but it was a real push to get the fourth. Overall, I feel that I have more peace of mind—but nothing profound. Struggles: As noted before, getting the fourth time in was a struggle. I also was not good at setting a schedule with the times since the weeks that I did the experiment were in the final semester of my school. To reiterate, I think the structure and process of the experiment is great, and it is a great tool to try to further your relationship with God. It was hard and frustrating to focus four times a

> day, but that falls on me as a person struggling to fit it in my crazy schedule. Overall, it was a good time and I would do it again.

Terry is a corporate executive for an international IT firm. He is married with adult kids. He writes:

> This is way harder than I thought. Not only do I have to be conscience of these timelines, but I also have to put them on a calendar or an alarm device, otherwise they pass me up. I couldn't limit it to two weeks. I have to continue now because you got me going on it. I have been listening for a while in my walk, but this adds a discipline to it all on purpose, as I would call it. Am I hearing differently? Jury is still out. Is my experience different? Still evaluating. For me when I do these things, I sometimes have to keep running tests. Still learning.

These are my personal observations and experiences from this experiment:

Doing this experiment was very challenging for me. Despite using alarms on my phone to remind me, I struggled. Sometimes the alarm went off at inconvenient times, like during a TV taping segment when I forgot to put it on silent, or while I was driving some place. Some days I forgot to turn my alarms on. I was grateful when Holy Spirit reminded me in the middle of the morning during a bathroom break about setting my alarms.

In the actual three minutes, at the beginning it took me longer to settle my thoughts into focusing on God. But the longer I practiced this, the easier it became. Eventually, I began to look forward to these pauses during the day. I found the pauses to be helpful reminders that God is present with me. I saw them as miniature retreats during busy days, as invitations to remember intimate moments and conversations with God, as opportunities for re-centering and refocusing on God, and as divine interruptions to recalibrate my focus and make perspective adjustments.

When I missed a three-minute pause, I struggled with feeling guilty. I felt like a failure, yet again. But I decided that continuing to try, despite my shortfalls, was better than giving up entirely. For me, this experiment gave me a glimpse and taste of what it could look like to be more focused on God throughout my daily living, regardless of schedules, appointments, responsibilities, deadlines, and distractions.

I liked that it was set up for a two-week experiment because I knew there was an end on the horizon. If I had felt like it was too much of a commitment, I would have worried that I would be unsuccessful. In conclusion, I want to do this experiment more consistently, such as doing it once a month with assessing and adjusting after each quarter.

I hope that you are encouraged from reading the feedback and observations from my friends who tried this experiment with me. I deeply appreciate their honesty and their willingness to express their struggles, pleasures, and discoveries with this adventure. To this end, I invite you to try this experiment. Keep track of what you feel and experience, and see how your conversation with God might deepen and expand beyond what you have known up to this point!

Enjoy!

For further reflection and note-taking see "Intentional Time" on page 248 in the Epilogue.

ENDNOTES

1. ProLiteracy, Mission/History; https://proliteracy.org/About -Us/Mission-History; accessed May 12, 2020.

2. Frank C. Laubach, *Letters by a Modern Mystic* (Colorado Springs, CO: Purposeful Design Publications, 2007).

EPILOGUE

As you have read through this book, it has been my hope and prayer that your conversations with God are increasing in a variety of ways—frequency, depth, breadth, continuity, and heaps more. I also pray that the Conversation Starters at the end of the chapters have been useful and eye-opening to you.

As we finish our time together, I would like to give some concluding thoughts that might be helpful to you with these Conversation Starters. Many of these Starters have come from a rich history and from a variety of sources as practiced by Christians throughout the centuries. I have practiced and experienced all of them in different ways and times over the course of more than twenty years.

As I have practiced these various Conversation Starters, I have also come to appreciate the balance among many tensions. These tensions include discipline, consistency, rigidity, vibrancy, seasons of life, mundane and flexibility, along with the ebb and flow of the daily responsibilities of raising children, work responsibilities, and travel.

Furthermore, it has been immensely helpful for growing in my conversations with God that I settle into one of these conversation methods over an extended period of time. For example, I have practiced the Praying in Holy Spirit Conversation Starter as a way of conversing with God on an almost daily basis for more than four years. The depth and transformation that these daily conversations have afforded me go far beyond my ability to describe. Suffice it to say that I am a wonderfully better person today than I was when I started this adventure a few years ago.

At the same time, it has been my experience that there can be a point in my life where a particular method of conversation can become dry, lifeless, mundane, and disconnected for me. When I have realized this place, it has been abundantly helpful to allow myself to explore a different way or method of conversing with God. Doing this has given me many rich and deep experiences with Him, enabling me to write about them for your consideration and possible practice.

I have also found it to be immensely helpful to write in a journal while sitting in a Conversation Starter. I am aware that I need to have some flexibility with the amount of time I have each day for the Conversation Starter I am using in that season. Sometimes I have more time because I have fewer demands and my nighttime sleep has been restful.

Sometimes I have less time because I have an extremely hectic day and/or my sleep the preceding night was restless, interrupted, short, or patchy. On the mornings when I do not get much quality, focused time with God, I ask Holy Spirit to help our conversation to be portable throughout that day. This has been really helpful.

The following are a few practical pointers that might also be helpful:

1. Do a Conversation Starter daily for at least four to six months to get comfortable with it. Let the conversation with God unfold over lots of time.

2. Do not hop around among these Conversation Starters with a consumer mindset looking for an immediate transactional benefit.

3. See each Conversation Starter as a springboard to grow into a more intimate relationship with God.

Finally, it is very important to give yourself some daily consistency in your conversations with God. When I first started intentionally conversing with God, I found it tedious to spend time together. My mind wandered to the day's events, to projects that I needed to finish, and to the emotional struggles I was wrestling with. As I have committed to a daily time with God, I have become increasingly settled in our conversations and intimate in our relationship. It has become my axiom that quality time with God equals genuine love—an existence essential for me to be the human of God's blueprint.

As I finish this epilogue, I want to leave you with a brief summary of each Conversation Starter. I am hopeful that these summaries will remind you about what you have read and that they will be a reference guide as you grow in your conversations with God.

EXAMEN [pg. 38]

This Conversation Starter is grounded in the Ignatius pattern and has five simple steps:

1. *Gratitude.* Reflect on your day, or the day before, looking for things about which you are grateful.
2. *Review.* Remember the day's events, looking for God's presence and fingerprints.
3. *Sorrow.* Recall the day, looking for conversations, actions, or attitudes where you feel remorse or regret.
4. *Forgiveness.* Ask for God's forgiveness for what brings sorrow or regret.
5. *Grace.* Ask for God's grace and an ability to see His presence more clearly in the real time of the day.

PRAYING WITH HOLY SPIRIT [pg. 59]

This Conversation Starter comes from the verbs associated with Holy Spirit's activities in Romans 8. I find it helpful to process these verbs in the order found in Romans 8 and to pause with each word for some possible dialogue with Holy Spirit around that verb.

1. Walk: Romans 8:4 – "*...who do not walk according to the flesh but according to the Spirit.*"

2. Think: Romans 8:6 – "*...but the mind set on the Spirit is life and peace.*"

3. Dwell: Romans 8:9 – "*...if indeed the Spirit of God dwells in you.*"

4. Make alive: Romans 8:11 – "*...will also give life to your mortal bodies through His Spirit who dwells in you.*"

5. Put to death: Romans 8:13 – "*...by the Spirit you are putting to death the deeds of the body....*"

6. Being led: Romans 8:14 – "*...being led by the Spirit of God....*"

7. Testify: Romans 8:16 – "*The Spirit Himself testifies with our spirit....*"

8. Help: Romans 8:26 – "*...Spirit also helps our weakness....*"

9. Intercede: Romans 8:26 – "*...but the Spirit Himself intercedes for us....*"

ACTION-BASED DIALOGUE [pg. 82]

This Conversation Starter is grounded and centered on some type of physical activity, letting the action occupy your body so that you can be free to converse with God. Some activities that can facilitate this Conversation Starter include daily walks, swimming, bicycle rides, treadmill walking, stretching, or weightlifting. Doing some physical activity over a quantity of time, like thirty minutes, is a great platform for dialoguing with God. It might be helpful at the end of the activity to write a log or a journal entry about the activity, the conversation, or what you might have felt or experienced with God. I have found that documenting the time can help the exercise be more tangible and memorable.

NAMES OF GOD [PG. 100]

This Conversation Starter centers on the names of God in the Old Testament as a way to help you know and converse with Him. It also can help you become grounded in God's character and nature. The following list is the names of God, along with a brief description and the biblical reference for that name. I have found it helpful to look at these names and let God direct me to one or two to talk about or explore in both reflection time and throughout the day's activities.

Elohim – Creator: Genesis 1:1 – *"In the beginning God created the heavens and the earth."*

El Elyon – God Most High: Genesis 14:20 – *"'And blessed be God Most High, who has delivered your enemies into your hand.' He gave him a tenth of all."*

El Roi – God who sees: Genesis 16:13 – *"Then she called the name of the Lord who spoke to her, 'You are a God who sees.'"*

El Shaddai – All Sufficient: Genesis 17:1 – *"Now when Abram was ninety-nine years old, the Lord appeared to Abram and said to him, 'I am God Almighty; walk before Me, and be blameless.'"*

Jehovah – Covenant Name of God: I am that I am: Exodus 3:14 – *"God said to Moses, 'I AM WHO I AM'; and He said, 'Thus you shall say to the sons of Israel, '"I AM has sent me to you."'"* This name was used the first time in Genesis 2:4 – *"This is the account of the heavens and* the earth when they were created, in the day that the Lord God made earth and heaven."

Jehovah Nissi – The Lord my banner: Exodus 17:15 – *"Moses built an altar and named it The Lord is My Banner."*

Jehovah Jireh – The Lord will provide: Genesis 22:14 – *"Abraham called the name of that place The Lord Will Provide, as it is said to this day, 'In the mount of the Lord it will be provided.'"*

Jehovah Raah – The Lord my shepherd: Psalm 23:1 – *"The Lord is my shepherd, I shall not want."*

Jehovah Rapha – The Lord who heals: Exodus 15:26 – *"And He said, 'If you will give earnest heed to the voice of the Lord your God, and do what is right in His sight, and give ear to His commandments, and keep all His statutes, I will put none of the diseases on you which I have put on the Egyptians; for I, the Lord, am your healer.'"*

Jehovah Shalom – The Lord is peace: Judges 6:24 – *"Then Gideon built an altar there to the Lord and named it The Lord is Peace."*

Jehovah Shammah – The Lord is present / there: Ezekiel 48:35 – *"And the name of the city from that day shall be, 'The Lord is there.'"*

Jehovah Tsidkenu – The Lord our righteousness: Jeremiah 23:6 – *"And this is His name by which He will be called, 'The Lord our righteousness.'"*

MEDITATIVE REFLECTION [pg. 121]

This Conversation Starter uses Bible verses as the starting point to converse with God. The following are a few verses I suggest:

- Psalms: 55:22; 16:8; 91:1; 143:9-10
- Jesus' Beatitudes: Matthew 5:3-12
- Moses' friendship with God: Exodus 33:11-13
- Paul's prayers:

  - Romans 1:8-10; 15:5-6,13
  - 1 Corinthians 1:4-9
  - Ephesians 1:15-23; 3:14-21
  - Philippians 1:3-6, 9-11
  - Colossians 1:3-14
  - 2 Thessalonians 1:11-12

These verses are just suggestions, and I suspect God will expand your horizons with many additional verses as you spend time exploring and practicing this Conversation Starter.

Here are the tips I suggested in this Conversation Starter that might be helpful to you:

- Start out with a small increment of time, like ten minutes. When you have built up some continuity with this method of conversation, you might consider increasing the amount in five-minute increments.
- Find a quiet place that has as few distractions as possible. This could be your car with the engine off,

an unused office or classroom at school, or a quiet room or space in your house, apartment, or living space.

- Put your phone on airplane mode to minimize interruptions.

- Have some paper and a pen readily available to write down what you hear and what is noteworthy. Additionally, using a paper and pen eliminates the temptation to use your phone for notes and the possibility of getting distracted by emails or text messages.

- Figure out a time in the day when you are alert and not sleepy for this kind of conversation.

- Be committed to trying this type of conversation for at least five days. This practice will create an honest experience that is not rushed or transactional.

- Be sure to use a Bible translation that is comfortable and engaging for you. Do not use a translation that is stiff, formidable, complicated, or difficult to absorb or ponder.

- Consider giving a friend permission to check in with you to confirm you are doing this conversation as a way of holding yourself accountable.

- Start each ten-minute practice with a prayer to God in which you ask for help to pay attention and to be present in the conversation.

LORD'S PRAYER [pg. 142]

This Conversation Starter uses the prayer that Jesus taught His disciples as a map for conversing with God, stopping at key topics—or levers—along the path for deeper dialogue. In Matthew 6:9-13 we read:

> *Our Father who is in heaven, hallowed be Your name. Your kingdom come. Your will be done, on earth as it is in heaven. Give us this day our daily bread. And forgive us our debts, as we also have forgiven our debtors. And do not lead us into temptation, but deliver us from evil. For Yours is the kingdom and the power and the glory forever. Amen.*

These are the levers I suggest in this Conversation Starter:

- **Lever 1:** Our Father who is in heaven
- **Lever 2:** Hallowed be Your name
- **Lever 3:** Your kingdom come
- **Lever 4:** Your will be done on earth as it is in heaven
- **Lever 5:** Give us today our daily bread
- **Lever 6:** Forgive us our debts as we forgive our debtors
- **Lever 7:** Lead us not into temptation but deliver us from evil
- **Lever 8:** Yours is the kingdom and the power and the glory forever

CREATIVE (VISUAL ART, MUSIC AND/OR WORSHIP, COOKING, MIXING SOUND, WRITING) [PG. 166]

In this Conversation Starter, we looked at the various contexts for creativity that can be used for having a dialogue with God. Consider reviewing the feedback in this Conversation Starter to inspire and encourage your own conversational exploration with creativity as the launch pad for this adventure.

_____

_____

_____

_____

_____

_____

_____

_____

_____

_____

_____

_____

_____

_____

_____

_____

LECTIO DIVINA [pg. 195]

In this Conversation Starter, I taught you how to look at a passage from the Bible to provide a focal point for your imagination and possible dialogue with God. You are to choose a collection of verses or a story to settle into, imagining yourself in that experience. These are the steps used in this Conversation Starter that are associated with *Lectio Divina:*

1. Relax and Attend (*silencio*) – to be quiet or silent
2. Read (*lectio*) – to read or absorb
3. Reflect (*meditatio*) – to meditate
4. Respond (*oratio*) – to reply (pray)
5. Rest (*contemplatio*) – to contemplate
6. Try it on (*incarnatio*) – to become incarnate

And here are some suggested passages to explore using this Conversation Starter:

- Jesus living in us: Ephesians 2:13-22
- Who is our neighbor: Luke 10:25-37
- Hearing God when life is discouraging: 1 Kings 19:3-18
- Fearfully and wonderfully made: Psalm 139:1-16
- When we fail: Matthew 14:22-33
- Wrestling with God: Genesis 32:24-32
- God loves you: Isaiah 43:1-7

- Changed identity: Luke 8:26-39
- Knowing God: Exodus 33:7-16
- What is important: Luke 10:38-42
- Love with action: James 1:19-27
- Spirit led living: Romans 8:5-17
- God hears you: Mark 5:24-34
- Being God's sheep: Psalm 23
- Be courageous: Joshua 1:1-9

INTENTIONAL TIME [pg. 214]

This final Conversation Starter is more of an experiment than a formal structure or system for conversation. In this experiment, I outlined the following steps and suggestions.

Giving God three minutes of undivided attention four times a day for two weeks—morning, noon, afternoon and bedtime, the same times every day for two weeks.

The following are some possible options to use during the three minutes:

- Requests to God
- Gives cares and/or worries to God
- Full focus on God (listen)
- Help with distractions
- Worship and glorify God
- Gratitude
- Inventory preceding hours for God's fingerprints
- Vulnerability: give God unrestricted access to emotions, desires, and assumptions

How would God converse with us? Suggestions:

- Resetting focus
- Giving comfort and consolation
- Giving input
- Directing observation
- Questioning perspective

- Fresh point of view

What I suggest: Document at least once a day what is happening during the experiment. How do you feel? What do you experience? Frustrations? Benefits? Document the cumulative effect of the experiment.

CONCLUSION

There are lots of ways to have conversations with God. Hopefully, these Conversation Starters have sparked your curiosity to explore and deepen your personal conversations with God. I am prayerful that your conversations with God will be ongoing, transformational, illuminating, encouraging, and, more than anything, that they will help you experience genuine love, because God is love—*"Beloved, let us love one another, for love is from God..."* (1 John 4:7).

ABOUT THE AUTHOR

Sarah Bowling is on a mission to connect everyone with the heart of God while living genuine love. Led by the Holy Spirit and anchored in the Word, Sarah seeks to inspire all to know the unconditional and transformational love of God in our daily lives. She is a discerning Bible teacher, an international speaker, and a global humanitarian. Sarah cohosts with her mother, Marilyn Hickey, a daily television program, *Today with Marilyn and Sarah*, reaching a potential daily audience of 2.2 billion households worldwide.

Visit the website: www.livinggenuinelove.org to stay current with her videos, blogs, events, and much more! Sarah has authored numerous books including: *How to Keep Your Faith in an Upside Down World; Hanging by a Thread: The Saving Moses Journey; Jesus Chicks; Heavenly Help; In Step with the Spirit; Jesus is God's Selfie;* and *Save Your Fork—There's More!*

Sarah is the founder of Saving Moses, a global humanitarian organization saving babies (five years and under) every day by meeting the most urgent and intense survival needs where help is least available. Saving Moses funds and establishes revolutionary programs in nations of the world that record the highest infant mortality rate and where babies of sex workers are most susceptible to exploitation. Visit the website at www.savingmoses.org.

Sarah and her husband, Reece, have three children and are lead pastors of Encounter Church in Denver, Colorado. She holds a Bachelor of Arts degree from Oral Roberts University and a Master of Arts degree from the University of Missouri.

Made in the USA
Middletown, DE
30 April 2021